Phonics to Teach Reading, Writing and Spelling

Kerry Dickinson

ISBN: 979-8-4602-2781-5

FOR MY MOM

PHONICS TO TEACH READING, WRITING AND SPELLING:

A HANDBOOK FOR THE TEACHING AND LEARNING OF PHONICS WITH IDEAS, DEFINITIONS, CHARTS, GAMES, AND ACTIVITIES FOR EYFS AND KEY STAGE ONE TEACHERS

CONTENTS

1 INTRODUCTION

There's only one thing I love more than teaching Phonics, and that's teaching about teaching Phonics. Phonics is the basis of speech and words and therefore books, reading and writing; it is the cornerstone of civilisation. It is quite literally the most important thing a child will ever learn at school as without the ability to read the child will be unable to learn anything else. It took many years of teaching, studying, reading, and learning to feel confident when teaching Phonics. When I started mentoring student teachers, I wanted a better way for them to learn and as a result wrote this book.

This book is written in the United Kingdom and uses the 2014 Primary National Curriculum in England as the framework within which the children are taught. The principles are the same worldwide, but the age the children learn to read and write may differ.

There are many excellent Phonics, spelling and reading products and programmes on the market; this is not one of those. This is a reference book for teachers and student teachers who need more knowledge to teach Phonics competently, confidently, and creatively.

This book begins with why we teach Phonics, the definition of Phonics and some key terminology. The teaching of reading and writing is sub-divided into six phases based on the *Letters and Sounds* document. In each phase, there is an explanation of the critical elements and advice on teaching that phase. There is a general outline of some learning difficulties and a basic lesson plan. The activities suggested are designed to engage children and are broken into visual skills, fine motor skills, phonological awareness, reading ideas, writing, and spelling activities and tasks to teach Tricky Words.

At the end of the book are various word lists as teacher reference material. They can also be used as a guide when deciding on spelling and reading lists. Included with the word lists are some spelling rules. Regional accents will dictate that certain words may not sound right phonetically in each phoneme/grapheme box; in this case, adjust the list to suit your teaching environment.

This book is for the teacher to use throughout the week to plan reading, writing, and spelling activities. Some of the ideas are quick and easy, and some require a little more preparation. Do not try to do everything; pick one or two new ideas a week and try those. You will soon find a few favourites that you revert to on a regular occasion. Children learn more when they are enjoying themselves, so be creative, be yourself and have fun.

2 WHY DO WE TEACH PHONICS?

Why do we teach Phonics? The simple answer is because it is the best way to learn to read and spell. An Australian study by Share (1984) concluded that the most reliable predictors of reading success was a child's phoneme segmentation abilities, while Lundberg (1980) and Parfetti (1987) believed that success depended on a child's ability to blend. In a synthetic-phonics programme, children are taught both the skills of segmenting and blending and become proficient readers from an early age.

The Jim Rose Review conducted by the UK government in 2006 found that most children will learn to read and spell using the synthetic phonics method. It is not a new method and has been used successfully in many schools both in the UK and abroad for many years but has only recently been a statutory method of teaching nationwide.

According to the Department for Education, schools should: "Present systematic, synthetic phonic work as the prime approach to decoding print." They should start learning Phonics daily in Reception in a sequential incremental manner. Children should be taught to recognise and blend sounds in English from left to right and should be taught through "Teacher-child interactions and involve a multi-sensory approach" (April 2021).

English is a relatively new language and comprises various root languages, including German, French, Greek, Saxon, and Latin. It is challenging for children to learn to read and spell in English. Many of the spellings have been retained from the original languages.

Traditionally children were taught to read words; however, the brain can only hold a finite number of whole words. Children also had a limited number of strategies to learn and read unfamiliar words. Children are given strategies to read unfamiliar words from the start with Synthetic Phonics. They are taught the structure and rules of words and can use this knowledge to read any word, significantly increasing their reading ability. Children are taught the sounds in quick succession and start reading early in the process, and this increases their confidence in their capabilities and helps build a love of reading.

Reading is an essential skill that dictates a child's future academic success. Phonics helps them to learn and understand that skill at an early age.

3 WHAT IS PHONICS?

We speak using sounds or phonemes, we spell using graphemes, and we read by linking phonemes and graphemes together in a meaningful way. Synthetic Phonics is a method of teaching spelling and reading by linking sounds to the letters that represent those sounds. The teaching of Phonics starts in the early years and does not end; there are always new rules to learn or words to read.

Sounds joined together when spoken form words; we call these sounds phonemes. In the word **bat,** there are three sounds joined together to make the word. The sound **b** is at the beginning of the word, **a** in the middle and **t** at the end of the word, so, **bat** has three sounds **b-a-t**, it has three phonemes.

Teach children to listen to the individual sounds in words. A child must recognise a letter (or group of letters), link those letters with sounds, and then join the sounds to read a word; dividing a word into its component sounds is called segmenting. Blending is when you say segmented sounds together to form a word. When reading the word **sheep,** the child will say the sounds **sh-ee-p** then join the sounds together to read the word **sheep**.

When we push sounds together to read a word, it called blending or synthesising, which is why this method of teaching is called Synthetic Phonics.

When children read, they:

- Read from left to right while converting letters to sounds.
- Blend the sounds.
- Pronounce the word.

When a child writes a word, they start with the whole word, and then they break the word into separate sounds. The child says the word **chip,** then sounds it out as **ch-i-p**; as they sound it out, they write down the letter representations for those sounds.

When children spell, they:

- Say the word.
- Identify the sounds from the beginning to the end.
- Write down the letter sounds from left to right.

It is imperative to teach reading, writing, and spelling together.

A grapheme is a letter or group of letters that represent a sound. Graphemes can consist of one to four letters. A grapheme that has one letter is called a graph. In the word **cat**, there are three phonemes because there are three sounds. **Cat** has three sounds, and three graphemes as the number of graphemes equal the number of phonemes; in the word **cat,** each grapheme is called a graph as they have only one letter.

In the word **paid**, there are four letters but three sounds and three spelling choices. The number of graphemes equals the number of phonemes. The graph **p** represents the initial sound, the graph **d** is the final sound, and the middle sound is made with two letters together to form the **ai** sound. Two letters together that make one sound is called a digraph.

A trigraph is a spelling choice formed by joining three letters together to make one sound. In the word **patch** there are three sounds. The graph **p** represents the first sound, the middle sound is the graph **a**, and the final sound **tch**, is formed using three letters, **tch** is a trigraph.

A four-letter spelling choice is called a quadgraph. Quadgraphs are rare and seldom need to be taught, but it is good to be able to identify and explain them. The word **eight** has two sounds; the initial sound is the quadgraph **eigh**, and the graph **t** represents the final sound.

In Phase Five, sounds that are spelt differently are called alternate spellings. For example, the **ai** sound can be spelt as ai in the word **train**, **a-e** in the word **cake**, **a** in **baby**, **ea** in **great**, **ey** in **grey** or **ay** in **play**.

The English alphabet consists of twenty-six letters; however, spoken English comprises forty-four or forty-six sounds depending on your language expert and regional accent. As a result, some sounds are created using a combination of letters known as digraphs, trigraphs and quadgraphs. The following sounds are the generally agreed upon sounds in the English language, along with the most common graphemes for each phoneme. The digraph **qu** is two separate sounds, but we teach it as one as it is challenging for young children to understand. The 'graph' **x** is also two distinct sounds, but we teach it as one sound to avoid confusion.

The Sounds in The English Language

Consonant Sounds	b	bird	Short Vowel Sounds	a	apple
	c/k	cat/key		e	egg
	d	dog		i	ink
	f	fish		o	orange
	g	goat		u	umbrella
	h	hat		oo	book
	j	jet	Long Vowel Sounds	ai	rain
	l	leaf		ee	tree
	m	mat		ie	tie
	n	nose		oa	oats
	p	pet		u-e	cube
	qu	queen		oo	spoon
	r	rat		oi	boil
	s	socks		ow	cow
	t	tap	Controlled R Vowel sounds	ar	car
	v	vet		ir	girl
	w	wet		or	order
	x	box		air	chair
	y	yellow		ear	beard
	z	zebra		ure	cure
	s	treasure			
Consonant Digraphs	sh	ship			
	ch	chip			
	th	feather			
	th	tooth			
	ng	king			

4 PHASE ONE- PRE-READING AND WRITING

The skills and experiences children need to become proficient readers are called pre-reading and writing skills and are referred to as Phase One in the *Letters and Sounds Document* (2007). Some of these activities may seem unrelated to reading but they all develop the child's listening, speaking and communication skills and their appreciation of stories and books. It is important to continue these activities after children have learnt to read to embed them and foster a love of reading.

Children must enjoy books and have positive experiences around reading before learning to read. They need to read with their grown-ups, listen to stories, go on trips to book shops and the local library, and explore books independently. All these activities inspire a child to want to learn to read.

There is a plethora of excellent children's literature to choose from, fairy tales or traditional tales as they are now called, are valuable for teaching the structure of stories. Religious stories help children learn shared values within a community and develop a better understanding of their faith. While stories from other religions develop a child's tolerance and understanding of different belief systems.

When children listen to books that contain rhyming words, they begin to recognise similarities and differences in words. Children love to join in with stories and may even predict the words in the story as they develop their understanding of rhyming words and expand their vocabularies.

Books containing alliterations highlight similarities and differences in sounds at the beginning of words. When you read these books, the children can think of other words that also start with the same sound and continue to deepen their knowledge of the sounds that make up words and the similarities and differences between words. Good picture books grab children's attention, they have interesting characters, excellent artwork, a good storyline, and twists in the tale. When reading picture books, remember to point to the text on the page as you read as this helps children to associate the words they can hear to the print on the page.

Books without text are also vitally important, with these books the adult or the child can make up the story as they go along, they can talk about setting, characters and actions and even compare stories. Storytelling is an ancient tradition going back thousands of years. These stories can be told without the aid of a book and will foster a child's love of stories and develop their imagination and understanding of plot. The children can contribute to the stories and decide on the characters, setting, twists in the tale or the ending.

Audiobooks improve children's listening skills. Some audiobooks come with picture books so that children can look at the pictures while listening to the story, these are particularly useful for younger children or children who struggle to focus without a visual aid. Listening to stories is a skill that takes time to develop but significantly impacts on a child's listening abilities. As a class teacher you may need to begin this activity with the aid of a book or for very short periods of time.

The classroom should be a word rich environment, and everything should be labelled including the furniture. As the teacher you can point out words and sentences everywhere and model reading. The children will soon start to read and recognise familiar words and symbols.

Good communication skills are vital to learning to read and write and adults should model speaking, listening, and turn-taking skills. Talk to children in complete sentences, use good vocabulary and avoid any baby language. Insist that children must use the right words for objects. Repeat words or sentences back to children correctly. For example, if Sarah says: "The doggy is black." Then say to Sarah: "Yes, I agree the **dog** is black."

If the child is in the habit of pointing at objects rather than using the words, then teach them the vocabulary and gently encourage them to vocally request things. For example, if you ask Tim what he would like to play with and he points at the teddy bear then you can say:" Would you like the teddy bear? This is called a teddy bear. Can you say teddy bear?" This way the child hears the phrase several times and hopefully says the word at least once and thus begins to develop both his receptive and spoken vocabulary. Give children plenty of time to speak, as sometimes it takes a child time to think of the words they need. Children learn through play; they are constantly communicating while playing and should be allowed as much time as possible for free play.

In Phase One, it is essential to develop a child's awareness of the sounds in their environment. Take the children for a listening walk, then have them stop and listen to what they can hear in the world around them. Use plenty of drama and intrigue when saying: "What can you hear?" The child then identifies what they have heard, a siren of a passing police car, an aeroplane flying overhead, or a dog barking in the distance and goes on to explain if it is near or far and maybe even makes up a story around what they have heard. Encourage to reproduce the sounds they can hear; this is lots of fun when playing pretend or dressing up. They can make siren noises, animal noises, weather noises or make up voices to accompany the characters in their play.

Playing instruments and music develops a child's awareness of sounds and their listening skills. Children need these skills to hear the sounds in words. Have noise makers available for free play and incorporate them into lessons. Instruments can be played loudly, softly, fast, slow, or simply just for fun. Have the children describe what they can hear while playing instruments.

Nursery Rhymes are a powerful teaching tool; they introduce children to new vocabulary, speech patterns, rhythm, and rhyme. They also develop memory and are an essential part of creating a cultural identity within the community. You can use body percussion while singing, acting out or saying rhymes to help children better remember the rhymes and develop their fine and gross motor skills. One rhyme can be done several different ways, you are only limited to your imagination and even then, Pinterest will take you into the realms of other teacher's imaginations. For example, for the Rhyme Insy Winsy Spider, the rhyme can be said loudly, softly, quickly, slowly or in different voices. You can take turns saying the different phrases in the rhyme or perform it as a round. You can paint spider and web pictures or research spiders. The children can do the traditional actions for the rhyme, they can do the actions as pairs or make up whole body actions for the rhyme. All these activities will develop the child's language, phonics, and vocabulary skills.

It is fun as the teacher to play with words and sounds; make up silly sounds or words, and have the children copy. Make up silly rhymes or words with the children or play word association games like, "I went to the zoo, and I saw..." Create rhyming strings in class and play "I spy" using the letter sounds.

The teacher models sound talking (sounding out words) and blending words throughout the day, 'Please put away your **b-a-g, bag**.' After a while, the children naturally begin hearing and blending the words themselves. You can then say: "Put away your b-a-g..." and the children can say "bag!" Only sound out the last word in the sentence; otherwise, it becomes confusing for young children. Avoid sounding out words with two consonants next to each, as these will be hard for the children to hear.

At this stage, the children have not been shown any letters or told what sounds they represent. This phase is about developing children's phonological awareness through oral games and having fun with words and sounds.

5 PHASE TWO - EARLY READING AND WRITING

In Phase One the vocabulary of language: words, letters, sentences, sounds, letter names were all used interchangeably. In Phase Two children start to distinguish between these terms and begin to understand the concept of words. Children begin to move from oral segmenting and blending activities to segmenting and blending with letters. They start to separate sentences into words, then words into syllables and lastly, words into sounds when writing and blend sounds into words and words into sentences when reading. It is a magical time for both the child and you as a teacher.

A child learns to recognise a letter (or group of letters) and link those letters with sounds to read a word, they then join (or blend) all the sounds in a word together. Children who have had a lot of practice with orally blending sounds find it easier to blend graphemes to read words.

In this phase, children learn nineteen different phonemes and their letter representations. They also learn that sometimes two letters make one sound. Do not teach these digraphs as something new or more complicated, simply different; children accept the idea and read the digraph **ll** as one sound and not as **l**, **l**.

The first stage in this process is learning the letter sounds. Begin by saying lots of words that begin with the new sound. Sing a song with the sound in it or tell a story containing words with the sound and have the children indicate, or do an action, when they hear the sound. Programmes such as *Jolly Phonics* encourage children to use actions for each sound; they have songs, stories, and activities suitable for teaching young children. An action linked to a sound can prompt a child when they are unsure of the sound. Show the children what the grapheme looks like and how to write the letter. Children usually hear the initial sounds clearly; they later develop the ability to hear to final sounds and later sounds within words.

It is best to introduce the letter name alongside the letter sound. "This is the letter **s** (name), and it makes the sound **s** (sound)." That way, there is no confusion when the child goes home and a parent or relative says the letter name. However, the emphasis should be on the letter sound. Review the letter names when you practice saying the alphabet. However, when using the flashcards, insist the children use the letter sounds as they need these when reading.

Most phonics programmes teach the sounds for the letters **s**, **a**, **t**, **p**, **i** and **n** first as these letters can make many two and three-letter words. These letters are also dissimilar from each other visually and audibly and, therefore, the most straightforward for children to distinguish. The letters **b** and **d** are in separate groups to reduce confusion.

Most consonant sounds can be said with an inflexion on the end, an inflexion is an "uh" sound; this extra sound is called a schwa. Pure sounds are the sounds that are said with as little a schwa as possible. When teaching children Phonics, try to make pure sounds to allow the child to hear the correct sound and blend the word correctly. The word **dog** can be sounded out as **duh-o-guh**; this results in the word **duhoguh**. However, when sounded out with pure sounds, the same word becomes **d-o-g** and can be blended to say **dog**.

Some children develop a habit of dragging out the sounds, particularly when reading flashcards. Encourage the children to say the sounds quickly and crisply; this will best facilitate reading when blending the sounds to form words as the child will be unable to hear the word being sounded out if each sound is dragged out.

When teaching children new sounds and their representations, have them observe you. For a voiced sound, they can feel the vibrations in their voice boxes by gently placing their hands on their throats while saying the sound. If the sound is unvoiced, they can put their hand in front of their mouths to feel the air escaping.

Voiced and unvoiced Sounds

Voiced Sounds		Unvoiced Sounds	
r	rat	**s**	sun
v	van	**f**	fan
d	dog	**k**	kit
g	goat	**t**	tap
s	pleasure	**p**	pot
z	zebra	**b**	box
b	bat	**ch**	chip
j	jet	**th**	thin
th	feather	**sh**	ship
l	leg	**h**	hat
m	man		
n	net		
All the vowel sounds			

In Phase Two children learn the single letter sounds and some consonant digraphs. They blend these to read words and segment them to spell words. Expose children to the sounds in different positions in words. The **s** sound can be at the beginning of a word (**sun**), in the middle (**lost**), or at the end (**pots**).

If a child can sound out the word and say the letter sounds but cannot blend them into a word, say the sounds with the child repeatedly, getting slightly quicker each time until they hear and say the word. If the child takes too long to recognise and articulate the sounds, they may not hear the word, so they must identify the sounds quickly and blend them with a degree of speed.

That is why there is a lot of emphasis on using flashcards and games requiring the child to recognise the sounds rapidly. Flashcards and oral blending practise should occur throughout the day and should not be restricted to the phonics lesson.

Blending and segmenting are skills that needs to be taught and modelled. At first, the child may need visual prompts like an action to recognise the letter sounds. Say the initial sound louder than the others when teaching children to sound out and blend words; this helps the child remember the initial sound. This is essential for a child that drops the initial sound when reading; they may say, **at** for **cat,** the child is blending but has either not heard or has forgotten the initial sound.

Words should be presented meaningfully within text or with pictures and not isolated on their own. Children start by reading VC (vowel, consonant) and CVC (consonant, vowel, consonant) words, as these are the most straightforward words for children to segment and blend.

Teach children the mechanics of reading. Show them how to read a word from left to right and point out the beginning and end of a word. Teach them that sounds joined together create words and words joined together sensibly make sentences. Show them that spaces separate words in a sentence and that a sentence begins with a capital letter and ends with a dot that we call a full-stop. They need to learn that we read from left to right and top to bottom. When modelling reading on the board, I always make massive sweeping movements with my arms to demonstrate while saying. "We read from the left to right and top to bottom" this quickly becomes a little chant that they learn and helps later when they are reading and writing.

Children should be given books to read from the start and these should be matched to the child's reading ability. A book that is too easy does not give the child a chance to develop their skills, while a book that is too difficult may make the child feel defeated and want to give up. In the early stages of reading, there should not be too many words on each page. Most of the words should be decodable with a few familiar Tricky Words. There should also be lots of repetition; this builds confidence and gives the child an opportunity to revise and assimilate new words.

Children are not expected to read every word in their book, they are guided through the book by an enthusiastic and encouraging adult. They can be asked to say the initial or final sound in the words or to sound out and read only the words they adult knows the child has the phonemic knowledge to read. They could read words that have obvious picture clues like the word dog under the picture of a dog. They can look for specific sounds or words in the book.

The adult points at the words as they read and encouraged the child to do the same, this helps reinforce the relationship between printed and oral words, develops the habit of reading from left to right and strengthens the child's visual tracking skills.

Informally assess children during the lesson. Regularly evaluate the children's ability to recognise and read phonemes. You as the teacher or a teaching assistant familiar with the phonics expectations can do an assessment with each child individually. Check both a child's aural recognition and visual recognition. If you say the sounds **b-a-t,** the child should say the word **bat**, and if the child sees the word **rat**, they should sound it out **r-a-t** and read the word **rat**. Keep each child's results in your reading or assessment file for reference purposes and keep a whole class checklist with all the children's names and the sounds they can recognise and blend; this allows you to see any sounds the entire class might be struggling with and reteach those sounds.

Phase Two Sounds

s	socks	a	apple	t	tap	p	pot
i	ink	n	nose	m	mouse	d	dog
g	goat	o	orange	c	cat	k	king
ck	duck	e	egg	u	umbrella	r	rat
h	hat	b	bat	f	fish	ff	muffin
l	leaf	ll	jelly	ss	hiss		

Segmenting is when children break up a word into different component sounds. The child says the word and then counts how many sounds they can hear on their fingers. For example, **rat**, **r-a-t**, **rat** has three sounds (phonemes). The child then writes each sound while the teacher watches to ensure they are writing from left to right. CVC words are the easiest to segment and write.

Teach children to write from left to right and top to bottom and observe them when they are writing; the finished word may appear to have been written backwards but, the child may have written the sounds in order but from right to left. Left-handed children tend to do this more than right-handed children.

In Phase Two, the emphasis is on hearing the sounds and writing down the sounds they can hear. Early writers may not hear all the sounds and may only hear the initial or the final sound; this is perfectly acceptable; encourage the child to write down what they can hear. If a child can only hear the first sound, then have them write that sound down. Help them hear the final sound by overemphasising the sound when you say the word. If they can hear and write the initial and the last sound, then over-emphasise the middle sounds to help them hear and write those sounds. If a child writes a phonetically plausible word, then the spelling is acceptable at this stage. A child trying to write the word **picture** may spell it **pikchu** this word is phonetically plausible as they have used their knowledge of phonics and made the correct phonemic choices but the wrong grapheme choices. With time, as the child learns more graphemes, is exposed to more text, and knows some spelling rules, their spelling will improve.

When writing a word, there are four steps; the child must:

- Say the word
- Count the sounds
- Write the word
- Check the word (They check if they used the correct number of sounds, if the sounds are in order and if the word makes sense.)

With time and lots of games developing their phonological awareness, their ability to hear the sounds and write words will improve. In the early stages, try to avoid consonant blends as these are particularly hard for children to hear.

Play games where children need to identify the position of the sound in a word such as:

- Where is **t** sound in **tap**?
- Where is the **t** sound in **pot**?
- Where is the **tt** in **butter**?

If a child says the sounds in a word but cannot retain them in their heads, then the teacher can remind them of what they have said or provide them with a voice recorder such as a talking tin. Some children can remember the sound and the letter associated but may need help remembering what the letter looks like; use a phonics chart to remind them of the letter formation. Sound charts are usually in phases, so the child will have access to the sounds they learn in class. A second chart sent home can be a valuable tool for parents when trying to help their child.

Short regular dictation sessions help children learn to write and spell. These must be fun, generally on the carpet with a whiteboard, and all the children should be encouraged to "Have a go." As the children begin to learn Tricky Words, the teacher can start to model and dictate some short captions and sentences. These are valuable formative assessment activities. Teach children to start a sentence with a capital letter, use finger spaces between words and end it with a full stop as soon as they begin writing sentences. Otherwise, bad habits could be difficult to break a few months or even years later.

Give children both formal and informal opportunities to write throughout the day. Provide different writing materials, surfaces, and environments in which to write. When writing is part of a child's surroundings, experience, and play, it becomes less intimidating.

Teach children to spell Tricky Words correctly. Tricky Words are commonly used words that are important for children to read to access simple texts but do not fall within the child's existing phonemic knowledge. As soon as children learn to read these words, they need to know how to spell them correctly. Show the child the "tricky" part of the word and the decodable part; this makes the word easier to remember and spell. For example, in the word **he**, the child knows the **h** sound and is shown that the letter **e** can make an **ee** sound. Tricky Words are Common Exception Words. The Tricky Words in Phase Two are: **the, to, I, no, go** and **into.**

Early reading and writing activities take place in Reception. However, some children may still be working on this stage in Year One and even Year Two; if this is the case, please see the chapter on reading and spelling difficulties.

6 PHASE THREE- DEVELOPING READING AND WRITING

In Phase Three children learn the remaining letters of the alphabet and some digraphs and trigraphs and is taught in Reception. Children find recognising digraphs and trigraphs in words difficult at first and will often sound out the word **rain** as **r-a-i-n** instead of as **r-ai-n**. However, most children will start seeing and reading digraphs and trigraphs in words with a bit of time and practice.

Children are now also exposed to decodable polysyllabic words early so that they do not develop a fear or avoidance of "Big words." Compound words are the most accessible polysyllabic words for children to read as you can teach children to chunk the word into smaller parts and then blend the chunks. For example, the word **cobweb** can be chunked into **cob by covering web** and **web** by covering cob and then blended to say **cobweb** when the whole word is revealed.

Phase Three Sounds

j	jelly	v	vet	w	wind	x	fox
y	yellow	z	zebra	zz	fizz	qu	queen
ch	chip	sh	ship	th	thumb	th	then
ng	king	ai	rain	ee	leek	igh	light
oa	goat	oo	moon	oo	book	ar	car
or	fork	ur	fur	ow	cow	oi	coin
ear	beard	air	chair	ure	cure	er	fern

Tricky Words are phonetically implausible words, they cannot be sounded out with the child's existing phonetic knowledge. However, these words frequently occur in text and therefore children need to learn to read and spell them to engage in language activities successfully. Teach these words as sight words, sight words are words that are learnt as a whole unit and are not sounded out. The Phase Three Tricky Words are **he, she, we, me, be, was, you, they, all, are, my** and **her**.

High-Frequency Words come up regularly in text; some of them are decodable, and some are not. Begin teaching children to read these words from Phase Three. A few of these words are also on the Tricky Words list; the *Letters and Sounds* document suggests teaching these words according to the frequency with which they occur. At the back of this book is a list of all the Tricky Words, High Frequency Words as well as Phase specific word lists.

7 PHASE FOUR – DEVELOPING SKILLS TO READ AND SPELL WORDS QUICKLY

Phase Four consolidates all the sounds taught in Phase Two and Phase Three. In Phase Four, children are also explicitly taught how to join two consonants alongside each other together. We call these consonant blends, and they can be difficult for children to hear. Words can have an initial consonant blend (**sweet**), final consonant blends (**hand**) or a combination of both (**stamp**). These words can also be referred to as CCVC words (consonant, consonant, vowel, consonant), CVCC words (consonant, vowel, consonant, consonant) or CCVCC words (consonant, consonant, vowel, consonant, consonant). In Phase Four, children read more polysyllabic words.

When teaching blends, tell the children that they will join two sounds together; my class calls them "Clicky" sounds because we click them together. For children to become fluent readers, they need to recognise and read consonant blends. Use flashcards and play quick recognition games to help children develop rapid recall. When children learn consonant blends, they then use them when sounding out unfamiliar words. For example, in the word **pump,** the final consonant blend **mp** can be chunked together, and the word sounded out as **p-u-mp**. Reading using consonant blends increases the child's chances of correctly hearing, reading, and spelling the word.

This phase is usually taught in Reception, however, if your class has particularly struggled to learn to read it may occur in early Year One.

Phase Four Blends

st	stone	nd	hand	mp	lamp	nt	tent
nk	ink	ft	gift	sk	skunk	lt	belts
lp	help	lf	elf	lk	milk	pt	script
xt	text	tr	tree	dr	drink	gr	green
cr	crab	br	brown	fr	frog	bl	blue
fl	flag	gl	glue	pl	plug	cl	claw
sl	sleep	sp	spoon	st	stop	tw	twig
sm	smell	pr	printer	sc	scarf	sk	skunk
sn	snail	nch	lunch	scr	scream	shr	shrimp
thr	three	str	string				

The Phase Four Tricky Words are **said, have, like, so, do, some, come, were, there, little, one, when out** and **what.** At the back of the book there is a consolidated word list for Reception. The list comprises Phase Two, Three and Four Tricky Words and Phase Two, Three and Four High-Frequency Words. The Phase Four Words are included in The Reception list as it is presumed the average class will complete Phase Four in Reception, however, if this is not the case then adjust the list appropriately.

8 PHASE FIVE - LEARNING TO READ AND WRITE UNFAMILIAR WORDS

In Phase Five children learn some new spelling choices and phonics vocabulary. A split digraph is when two letters together make one sound but are separated by a consonant; **a-e, e-e, u-e, o-e,** and **u-e** are the five split digraphs. Split digraphs used to be taught as "magic e" words. When you add a "magic e" on the end of the word it changes the short vowel sound in **pin** to a long vowel sound to make the word **pine.** When children first start learning about split digraphs, they should presume that any word ending in an e is a split digraph and use the long vowel sound.

Some sounds can be made using different graphemes, and some of the same spellings make different sounds, this is due to origins of the word, these are called alternatives. In Phase Five, children learn to identify alternative graphemes (same sounds with different spellings) and alternative phonemes (same spellings for different sounds). For example, the **ai** sound in **rain** can also be represented with **eigh** for **eight**, **ey** for **grey**, **a-e** for **cake** or **ay** like in the word **day,** these are alternative spellings (graphemes) for the same sound (phoneme). The spelling(grapheme) **y** can make different sounds (phonemes) such as in the words **pony, sky, yacht,** and pyramid. Children accept this idea easily and begin to ask questions such as "Which **ai** must I use?" These alternatives are often grouped into sounds.

Regularly remind the children of the alternative graphemes and phonemes; this will help them read and spell unfamiliar words. I like to put stickers, one per sound, on flashcards to remind myself and the children of all the different sounds that a grapheme can represent. So, for example, on the digraph flashcard **ea** I put two stickers on the front to remind me that **ea** can make the sound **ee** sound in the word **bead** and the **e** sound like in the word **bread**; this also helps the children get used to the idea that one grapheme can have more than one phoneme and vice versa.

For vowel graphs try the short vowel sound before the long sound as the short sound is more common. When children encounter an unfamiliar word, they try the first phoneme choice (the most common one) and if that does not work, they try another phoneme choice. For example, if they encounter the word **spread** for the first time, they read the **ea** grapheme with the long sound and then try the short sound and decide which pronunciation sounds right. They quickly learn the mantra, "If it (the sound) doesn't work, try, try another way."

I also write lists of words on the back of the flashcards, so that I always have example words available to use in my lessons. At the end of quickly flashing through the flashcards at the beginning of a phonics lesson I will have a child pick a card from the pack of flashcards, everyone then says the sounds that the grapheme choice represents, I then select a word from the word list on the back of the card, and the children write the word on their whiteboards. I normally pick two or three different words with different sounds so that they get used to spelling words with different sounds with the same grapheme. For example, if the child picked the grapheme **a**, I might ask the children to spell **anthill, bath, baby, pizza,** and **wasp**.

Phase Five Vowel Sound

ur	fur	**ai**	rain	**or**	storm	**air**	chair
ir	bird	**eigh**	weight	**our**	pour	**are**	mare
ear	pearl	**ey**	grey	**aur**	dinosaur	**ear**	pear
er	stern	**a-e**	snake	**aw**	saw	**ere**	where
or	worm	**ay**	play	**al**	walk	**aer**	aeroplane
our	journey	**ei**	reindeer	**au**	haunted		
		ea	great	**ough**	bought		
		e-e	fete	**ore**	sore		
		ae	sundae	**oor**	door		
		a	baby	**augh**	daughter		
ow	cow	ear	fear	ar	car	oi	coin
ou	house	eer	deer	al	calf	oy	toy
ough	drought	ere	sphere	a	bath	uo	buoy
		ier	pier				
u-e	cube	u	umbrella	er	letter	i	pin
u	uniform	o	won	ar	collar	y	pyramid
ew	dew	oo	flood	or	doctor	e	rocket
ue	argue	ou	enough	a	pizza	ui	guitar
oa	goat	oo	moon	ee	green	igh	light
oe	toe	ew	chew	y	pony	i	lion
o	no	u-e	cube	e-e	even	ie	pie
ow	throw	ue	blue	ey	key	i-e	pine
o-e	bone	ui	fruit	ea	bead	y	sky
ough	dough			ie	thief		
				e	me		
oo	book	e	bed	o	orange	ure	pure
u	bull	ea	bread	(w)a	wasp		
				ho	honest		

Phase Five Consonant Sound Families

c	cat	ch	chip	l	leg	t	tap
ck	sock	tch	watch	ll	hill	tt	mitt
k	king	t	picture			th	Thomas
ch	school					ed	jumped
qu	croquet						
cc	acclaim						
f	fish	j	jelly	m	mouse	n	nest
ff	waffle	g	giraffe	mb	lamb	kn	knight
ph	dolphin	gg	exaggerate	mn	Autumn	gn	gnome
gh	cough	dge	bridge	mm	hammer	nn	bunny
ft	often	gy	gym			pn	pneumonia
		di	soldier				
		ge	cage				
ng	king	r	rat	s	sun	sh	ship
n(k)	sink	rr	barrel	ss	kiss	ch	chef
ngue	tongue	wr	wrist	sc	scissors	ss	tissue
		rh	rhyme	ce	ice	ti	station
				ps	psyche	ci	suspicion
				st	listen	s	sugar
				ci	city	si	mansion
v	vet	w	wet	h	hat	b	bat
ve	give	wh	whistle	wh	whole	bb	rabbit
		u	queen				
d	dog	g	get	z	zebra	y	yacht
dd	middle	gg	egg	zz	buzz	i	opinion
ed	filled	gh	ghost	ze	amaze	j	hallelujah
		gu	guest	se	rose		
		gue	catalogue	s	bends		
				ss	scissors		
				x	xylophone		
p	panda	s	treasure				
pp	hippo	si	division				

Children also encounter homographs in Phase Five; homographs are spelt the same but pronounced differently. Children read the sentence to understand the context of the word and then pronounce the word correctly.

Tricky Words are commonly used words that children need to learn to read to access simple texts, but they do not fall within the child's existing phonemic knowledge. As soon as children learn to read these words, they also need to know to spell them correctly. The Phase Five Tricky Words are **oh, there, people, Mr, Mrs, looked, called, asked** and **could.**

In Year One, children learn to read and spell the Year One Common Exception Words, these words are phonetically implausible, and some of these will already have been learnt as Tricky Words in

Reception. At the back of the book is a combined word list for Year One. It comprises of Phase Five Tricky Words, Phase Five High-Frequency Words, the Year One Common Exception Words and the first 100 High-Frequency Words. All the words that appear in the previous phases or year are not included in the list to make the lists more coherent.

Graphemes with Alternative Phonemes

a	apple	what, bath, acorn
c	cat	ice
e	egg	he
g	goat	giraffe
i	ink	mind
ie	tie	thief
o	orange	no, mother
s	socks	sugar, cheese, treasure
t	tap	picture
u	umbrella	pull, unicorn
ue	blue	value
y	yellow	fly, berry, gym, python
oo	book	spoon
ar	car	warm
er	fern	teacher
or	order	work
ch	chip	school, chef
th	this	thin
wh	wheel	whole
ow	cow	snow
ear	beard	wear, learn
o-e	note	come
e-e	these	here, there
u-e	cute	rude
al	calf	call, capital
our	four	colour
se	house	please
ey	donkey	obey
ew	newt	grew
ea	peanut	head, great
ough	bought	plough, rough, dough, through
ui	biscuit	bruise
ou	cloud	soup, mould, could
ere	sphere	where
our	pour	odour

9 PHASE SIX- BECOMING A FLUENT READER AND WRITER

In Phase Six, children read words on sight without segmenting and blending out aloud. Most segmenting and blending will occur in the child's head with little need to sound out audibly. The child will understand the mechanics of reading and should be developing greater fluency. As children become more competent readers, they become more confident and begin to read and write for pleasure.

Good readers have the skills needed to read any unfamiliar word they encounter by segmenting the word and then blending those sounds correctly to say the word. They recognise when a word does not sound right and use other sound choices until they have read the word correctly. They use sentence context to help them ascertain the meaning of an unfamiliar word and predict what the next word or sentence is in a paragraph. Good readers are not only automatic decoders of words. Instead, they use the expression, vary their pace, change their tone, volume, and inflexion to capture their audience's attention.

Good writers have a knowledge of the different graphemes available for different sounds and some of the spelling rules used to determine the correct grapheme choice. Their spelling is phonetically plausible and often correct, they spell common exception words and Tricky words correctly. They use of capital letters, full stops, exclamation marks and question marks correctly, their sentence make sense and they check their writing. Good writers write for an audience, they make thoughtful word choices, can improve their writing, and use writing devices such as adjectives, adverbs, and expanded noun phrases to make their writing more interesting.

It is vital to teach comprehension skills at this stage and encourage them to think about the text, question what they have read, and make inferences. The child has learnt to read, and now they read for learning. Therefore, comprehension skills, inference skills and thinking skills are the focus of guided reading lessons in this stage. Greater Depth readers will be able to think, talk and write about what they have read in an intuitive and meaningful way.

In Phase Six, children need to understand how to read and write in different tenses. They learn to change the meaning of words by adding prefixes and suffixes to root words. They learn more complex spelling rules and how to change the function of words. Children are introduced to homophones in Phase Six. Homophones are words that sound the same but are spelt differently. They also revise homographs: words that are spelt the same are pronounced differently and have different meanings.

Children start understanding morphology in Phase Six. A morpheme is the smallest complete part of a word. A free morpheme is a whole word, usually called a root word, while a bound morpheme is a suffix or prefix. An understanding of morphemes helps children read and spell unfamiliar words. In addition, an understanding of the meaning of the separate parts of a word, this helps children spell and understand new words. For example, knowing that the **dec**, when used as a prefix, means ten can help children deduce the meaning of **decade** and **decagon** as well as spell these words.

I like to teach morphology using a tree as a visual aid. The root word is the root of the tree, and these root words can grow and change by adding prefixes or suffixes onto the words they then grow into new words. As we learn new prefixes and suffixes, we add these as leaves onto the trees so that they can be used to change root words. We also add common root words to the base of the tree such as write, happy, cry, true, tie, fear and usual. With time children start to use these words in the writing making their writing richer and more interesting. For children to be considered greater depth writers at the end of Year Two one of the criteria is that they use prefixes and suffixes in their individual writing, so it is worth taking the time to teach this concept thoroughly.

Prefixes: come before the root word
re: rewrite

Suffixes: come after the root word
er: writer
ing: writing
s: writes

Root Word: is the main word
write

In Year Two, children learn to read and spell the Year Two Common Exception Words. At the back of the book is a consolidated word list for Year Two; this comprises the Year Two Common Exception Words and the following 100 High-Frequency Words. Any of the words that appear in the previous years are not included in the list to make the list as coherent as possible.

10 THE PHONICS SCREENING

The Phonics Screening Test is a statutory standardised government-issued attainment test that ascertains a child's ability to recognise and blend sounds to read words to the desired level. The test is changed every year and covers the first five phases.

The test is sent to the school and then kept securely locked away. Once the test has been administered it is important to maintain the confidentiality of each child's score. The test starts with easy words and gets progressively harder. It is a combination of actual words and "alien" words. Alien words are made up words that are phonetically decodable. The inclusion of alien words tests whether children can phonetically decode and read unfamiliar words. Alien words have a picture of a little alien next to them, so the child knows they are nonsense words. Some children, particularly those on the autistic spectrum find alien words particularly difficult.

You as the child's teacher or another familiar teacher administer the test on a one-to-one basis with each child. Practice tests are held in the months running up to the screening; these monitor the child's progress and give them exposure to the process so that the child does not experience anxiety. There is no time limit to the test, and the child's speech and accent are taken into consideration. Teachers are given online training before administering the test and are subject to moderation, so the process is as fair as possible.

All children are expected to sit the screening, but the teacher may stop the test if she feels the words are too hard for the child. The department gives excellent guidance on administering the test, and teachers are expected to be familiar with this. Children with SEND should be allowed to do the test. Coloured overlays can be used, and the font can be adjusted online.

If the test is going to be administered with the test book provided, then use the same font in phonics lessons as many children read the letter **i** as a **j** in the test because of the font. When preparing for the test, insist that children sound out and blend all the words presented in the phonics screening format, even if they think they know the word. Good readers sometimes presume they know the words and then get them wrong. They do not need to do this when reading, just for the screening practices and the screening itself.

Children love the experience and do not feel any pressure around the testing process. Parents are given the results after the pass mark is released, and the data is submitted to the Department for Education. Children who do not pass the screening will redo the screening in Year Two. The pass mark has been thirty-two out of Forty for a few years now, but this is subject to change and is only made official after the screening.

11 READING AND WRITING DIFFICULTIES

If a child is falling behind and not learning to read and write at the same pace as other children, the first thing to do is to find out what the child does know; this is done on a one-to-one basis by the teacher or someone confident in assessing Phonics. Children who are struggling to learn to read must read daily in school. They should stay with the class for phonics lessons, and phonics interventions should occur at another time, so the children are still exposed to good quality phonics teaching and do not fall further behind. A child struggling to learn to read and write may struggle with memory or processing difficulties, auditory difficulties, visual difficulties, poor fine motor control or a specific learning difficulty such as Dyslexia.

Memory or Processing Difficulties

Children struggling to learn to read may have trouble with memory or processing speed. Processing speed is the speed it takes to complete a task with reasonable accuracy. Some children may battle to concentrate and focus. These children will benefit from working in a small group in a quiet area.

Some children may need some of the sounds re-taught before moving on to new sounds. When a child has blended a word, they should recognise the word and read it automatically. Explain to the children that they can say it if they know the word and do not have to sound it out. Children should only sound out and blend unfamiliar words (unless they are practising for the phonics screening). Some children take longer to recognise whole words, and they will need more repetition.

Auditory Difficulties

A child struggling to hear phonemes may have a hearing problem and should have a hearing test. If the child has good hearing, they may have auditory perceptual difficulties; they may be struggling to understand or distinguish what they are hearing. Children with auditory processing difficulties may appear not to listen, often look confused, take a long time to complete tasks, misunderstand instructions, or ask things repeatedly. Auditory problems may comprise of one or more of the following challenges:

- Auditory Discrimination: This is the ability to distinguish between different sounds in the environment.
- Auditory Sequencing: This is the ability to recall words or sounds in order.
- Auditory Memory: This is the ability to recall what has been heard.
- Auditory Figure-ground Discrimination: This is the ability to focus on the essential sounds in a noisy environment.

Some children struggle with blending and as a result, they may try to remember whole words. Go back to the pre-reading stage and start by segmenting and blending orally without letters to develop the child's auditory skills and then with letters. Auditory segmenting and blending can be modelled and practised throughout the day.

Play sound games with the child, say the sounds, and see if the child can blend the sounds to say the word. For example, say **sh-ee-p** and see if the child can hear and say the word **sheep**; do not give them any visual clues; this is a test to see if children can hear the sounds and blend them. Repeat the process in reverse with new words to see if a child can segment the word into its parts, say the word **ship**, and the child should say **sh-i-p**; this is a vital skill for spelling.

The child may have a short short-term auditory memory and struggles to retain the sounds heard or learnt. This child needs to play lots of auditory games to develop listening skills and memory. Play word games like the "I went to the store and bought."

Help children with short auditory memories to blend longer words by teaching consonant blends; this reduces the number of sound chunks a child needs to remember and increases their chances of success.

Visual Difficulties

Visual perception is the child's ability to make sense of what they see; a child may have perfect vision but still struggle with visual perception. Children who struggle with visual perception may look disorganised; they mislay things often and find it difficult to copy from the board. They may reverse numbers and letters and struggle to make their letters the correct size when writing. They find it hard to remember sight words and often lose their place when reading. They have difficulty recognising the graphemes taught and struggle to see those graphemes in words. Visual Perceptual problems may comprise of one or more of the following challenges:

- Sensory Processing: This is the child's ability to interpret the messages he/she is receiving from their senses.
- Visual-Spatial Relationships: Understanding where things are in space and in relation to each other.
- Visual Attention: The ability to focus on important information visually.
- Visual Discrimination: This is the child's ability to see similarities and differences.
- Visual Sequential Memory: This is the child's ability to remember objects in order.
- Visual Figure-Ground: This is the child's ability to find something on a busy background.
- Visual Form Constancy: This is the child's understanding that a shape or letter remains the same despite its size or orientation.
- Visual Memory: This is the child's ability to remember an object visually.

Ensure that children who struggle with visual perceptual difficulties have clean, clutter-free desks and that their worksheets are straightforward without unnecessary decoration. Seat these children in a quiet part of the classroom with few visual distractions from busy, colourful displays. Keep the classroom as clutter-free as possible and put equipment away in cupboards or drawers.

Test the child's eye-tracking ability; the ability for the child to move their eyes along a line of text smoothly when reading. A simple check for this is to have the child hold their arm straight in front of them, keep their head still and then have them move their arm in large figures of eight while watching their thumb. If the child moves their head to do this, or you notice their eyes bouncing, then they are struggling with tracking. There are simple exercises to help develop a child's eye muscles such as putting a toy car on the table and driving it from left to right, returning, and repeating the action, the child watches the car with his eyes while keeping his head still. Always allow children to use their fingers or a bookmark to follow along the line when reading; this is not poor reading; on the contrary, it develops fluent readers with good tracking skills.

If children are struggling with visual difficulties, the first specialist is an optometrist. Other specialists you may consider are Occupational Therapists and Vision Therapists.

Poor Fine Motor Control

Some children may segment words correctly and yet are not making progress with their writing. Children with fine motor difficulties will struggle to hold a pencil and to colour or draw neatly. They avoid using scissors and tasks such as threading, using large tweezers or doing up buttons. They dislike construction toys and are slower to learn self-care tasks. They have poor posture and tend to tire quickly and lie on the desk.

Poor fine motor skills may consist of one or more of the following difficulties:

- Crossing the Midline: This is the child's ability to cross the invisible line that runs from the top of the head down through the middle of the body through the nose.
- Finger and hand strength: The physical strength in the hands.
- Hand Dominance: The consistent use of one preferred hand for repetitive tasks.
- Bilateral Integration: The ability for the two hands to work together to perform a task, like holding a piece of paper with one hand and cutting with the other.
- Object Manipulation: The ability to use tools like scissors, a hairbrush, and pencils effectively.
- Postural Control: This is the child's ability to hold themselves upright through the trunk.
- Shoulder Stability: The shoulder strength and control needed to perform fine motor tasks.

These children need lots of activities to develop their fine motor control. Help the child establish hand dominance by watching to see which hand they favour and then encouraging them to use that hand for tasks. Demonstrate using two hands to complete activities, for example, holding a piece of paper with one hand while cutting with the other. Encourage play with activities that require fine motor control and strength, such as construction toys, threading, painting, and playdoh. Provide lots of opportunities for craft and cutting tasks. The most popular fine motor activity I have ever had is small world animals wrapped in elastic bands, and the children try to free the animals from the elastic bands.

Consult Occupational Therapists for children whose fine motor difficulties as these will affect their ability to make progress in their learning.

Dyslexia

Dyslexia is a neurological learning difficulty. It consists of problems in auditory processing, phonological awareness, executive function, processing speed and working memory. Every person with Dyslexia presents slightly differently as they have different combinations of strengths and weaknesses. **However, the main difficulty with Dyslexia is reading.**

Children who struggle with Dyslexia may present with the following difficulties:

- Struggles with Phonics.
- Poor handwriting.
- Trouble remembering sight words.
- Lose their place when reading.
- Forget punctuation.
- Struggle to stay on task.
- Often lose things and are disorganised.
- Poor spelling.
- Leaves out, inserts, or guesses words when reading.
- Slow reading.

- Ignores or mixes up suffixes.
- Trouble with rhyming.
- Confuses the sequence of letters when writing or reading.

Children are usually only tested for Dyslexia from age seven but present with the symptoms from a young age. These children need multi-sensory learning experiences. Base new learning on previous knowledge. The teaching of Phonics needs to be explicit and carefully planned. Use word families, mnemonics, and picture association to help children learn to spell. If by Year Two the child is still struggling to learn to read and spell, then it may be time to start considering learning difficulties such as Dyslexia. Formal testing for Dyslexia usually occurs around the year the child turns seven, so we start looking at it in Year Two.

Children with Dyslexia may benefit from vision therapy, speech and language therapy, occupational therapy, and chiropractic care. Provide them with off white paper to work from to reduce visual stress, left align font and make the letters larger. Pre-teach and over-teach all language-based activities. Allow plenty of time for activities and tests. Teach in a multi-sensory way and provide the child with other ways to show their knowledge like drawing or talking about what they know.

Dysgraphia

Children need to learn to write with automaticity early on; this means that the child will not need to consciously think about producing every letter. Children should have developed this skill by Year Two to focus their mental energy on more complex language tasks. However, children with Dysgraphia struggle to learn to write letters, words, and sentences. These children may be labelled messy or lazy. It is a combination of difficulties involving fine motor control and visual processing. **The main difficulty with Dysgraphia is writing.**

Children with Dysgraphia show the following signs:

- Difficulty forming letters.
- An unusual pencil grip or handling of craft equipment.
- Tires when writing and complains of hand pain.
- Avoidance of fine-motor activities.
- Difficulty staying on the lines when writing.
- Difficulty spacing letters in words and words in sentences.
- Letter and number reversals.
- Slow, laborious writing pace.
- Oral communication is far better than written communication.
- Struggles with sentence structure.
- Poor punctuation.

Occupational therapy, vision therapy, speech and language therapy and chiropractic care can be effective in helping children with Dysgraphia. Extend the time available for tasks and tests. Practise writing using sensory writing activities and develop a child's keyboard skills to reduce the need for writing.

Dyspraxia

Dyspraxia is a medical condition that affects the movement of both fine and gross muscles. Children are diagnosed with Dyspraxia from the age of five onwards.

Children with Dyspraxia show the following signs:

- Difficulty with balance, coordination, and movement.
- Struggle to learn self-care tasks such as dressing and eating with cutlery.
- Trouble managing emotions and behaviour.
- Poor time management and planning.
- Handwriting difficulties.
- Immature speech and poor listening skills.
- The child looks clumsy.

Dyspraxia is diagnosed by a team of specialists, including psychiatrists, neurologists, physiotherapists, and paediatricians, as DCD (Developmental Coordination Disorder). Specialist treatment for Dyspraxia includes occupational therapy, chiropractic care and cognitive behavioural therapy: Pre-teach and over-teach physical skills. Provide lots of opportunities for children to play, swim, use the play trail and engage in active play outside.

Involving Parents in A Child's Progress

If a child is struggling to learn to read or to spell age-appropriately, speak to the parents. Most parents would rather know sooner as they can then intervene and help early in the reading and writing process before their child falls too far behind. Tell the parents what the child can and cannot do and give them something they can do at home to help. This help is invaluable as parents can provide the child with one-to-one support, which is seldom available in school.

Children without severe learning difficulties may not get all the help they require in school as it is impossible to provide for all the different struggles children may have within the school environment from an expertise, budget or staffing perspective. For that reason, I often tell parents about private specialists such as Vision Therapists, Occupational Therapists, Speech Therapists and Dyslexia Assessors. Parents are grateful for the information and feel empowered knowing they can do things to help and places they can go for support. Do not be afraid to recommend specialists (provided your school policy allows you to do so) if a child goes for an assessment and it comes back that nothing is wrong, that is also good news as it rules out one possibility, and you can then look at other potential reasons for their struggles.

12 LESSON PLANS

Essential Terminology

Lesson Objectives

Lesson objectives are **what** the children are learning and **how** this will be assessed. The lesson objectives should be written in a sentence and should contain an action verb. The following six verbs taken from Blooms Taxonomy; **remembering, understanding, applying, analysing, evaluating,** and **creating**, are helpful as they assist both the children and the teacher in measuring the effectiveness of the lesson (Kelly, 2020). Share the lesson objective with the children at the start of the lesson as this helps them understand what they are learning and why. There can be more than one lesson objective for the lesson; however, small children will struggle to retain and understand multiple lesson objectives. Multiple lesson objectives can also muddle your teaching as one clear outcome is easier to teach towards.

Curriculum Links

The curriculum links are the subjects taught in the lesson and the skills, knowledge, and standards within that subject; these are set out in the National Curriculum. There may be more than one curriculum link for the lesson. Curriculum links together with the lesson objectives help direct and plan the lesson. Cross-curricular links are when there is more than one subject being covered in the lesson. For example, a writing lesson may focus on writing a historical recount, in which case there would be curriculum links to both English and History.

Resources

Resources are all the things needed for the lesson. Carefully think about the resources list; any problem with resources will result in lesson disruption and behaviour issues. List the PowerPoint, the stationery for the teacher and children, and any teaching and learning aids. It is also a good idea to write down how you are deploying support staff, specific instructions for those staff and their objectives.

Revise

Revise all prior learning or find out from the children what they already know. If the children have little prior knowledge, you will need to teach the information they are missing; if they have a good understanding of the topic, adjust your lesson to reflect their knowledge. If the class is too hard or too easy, behaviour problems may result from frustration or boredom.

Teach

Explicitly teach the new knowledge or guide the children towards discovering the information for themselves. Do not spend too much time on this section of the lesson as children may get fidgety and lose concentration. Teach concepts in short, easy to understand chunks. When explicitly teaching a new concept to little children, use the phrase: "My turn…" before modelling the learning.

Supported Practice

Supported practice is when the children practice the new information with the support of the teacher. They can practically engage in an activity or work on a whiteboard or in a jotter. Encourage partner talk, small group work and collaboration during this stage as children need to communicate to understand what they are learning; this should be a low stakes activity. The children should feel free to participate without the fear of failure; this is an excellent opportunity to ascertain any misconceptions and address these. For young children use the phrase; "Our turn…" during this stage of the lesson.

Application

The application part of the lesson is the part of the lesson where children apply what they have learnt, use the phrase "Your turn…". Children may work in small groups, independently or be supported by an adult. During this stage of the lesson, the teacher guides and monitors the children's learning but tries not to interrupt and disturb them. They need time to think and communicate their ideas, and constant interruptions can disrupt their learning. Allow plenty of time for children to explore and embed their learning.

Ability Grouping

Children can be grouped in different ways depending on the outcome of the lesson. Group children according to ability to ensure that they can access the work and provide differentiated activities. Always consider and differentiate for SEND learners so that they can access the learning in a meaningful way. Keep children in the same groups for a series of lessons, or group them for particular lessons based on their needs and skills. Regularly evaluate groups and move children as their needs and abilities change.

Non-ability groups can encourage lower ability children to work at a higher level and higher ability children to help and teach other children, which allows them to develop mastery.

Children may want to choose their groups; this gives valuable insight into their planning and organisational skills and their friendship groups and social skills.

Plenary

The plenary is when the teacher stops the lesson, gets the children's attention, reviews the lesson objectives, consolidates new knowledge, addresses any misconceptions, or moves the learning forward. It is usually at the end of the lesson; however, it can also be mid-way through the lesson if the teacher thinks there is a better time to stop and address the class. Try not to make the plenary a dry mini lecture on the lesson. Good plenaries get the children involved, use questioning techniques, allow for reflection and communication, show examples of good work, have a quiz, or play a game.

Give me five is a good example of an interactive plenary: The children hold up one finger for each question/answer, and the teacher asks.

1. What have you learned in this lesson?
2. What skills have you used?
3. What did you find tricky?
4. What did you get better at?
5. What do you need to remember for next time?

Assessment

Assessment can be formative, summative or both. Formative assessment is evaluating the children's ability and understanding while they are learning. The teacher observes the children, asks questions and evaluates their work. Formative assessment is also known as Assessment for Learning as it helps the teacher decide on the child's next steps in their learning and is an ongoing activity. Summative assessment is the assessment of children's learning at the end of a unit. It is usually a piece of independent work or a test; this is generally evaluated against a benchmark to determine the child's attainment level.

Next Steps

At the end of the lesson, the teacher notes what went well and what could have gone better. Reflects on your practice as well as the children's learning. This knowledge helps guide and direct planning for subsequent lessons. The next steps can be child or group-specific or applicable to the whole class.

Intervention

Teach small group interventions using the same lesson format as a whole class lesson. Use a variety of resources to keep the children interested and enthusiastic. The adult in charge should use pure sounds and do good modelling. Make use of plenty of repetition and correct misconceptions

A Phonics Lesson Teaching the oa Sound		
Subject: English	Year group:1	Date:
Lesson Objectives To understand and remember how to read and write the **oa** sound in words.	Curriculum Links English-Reading-Word reading: apply phonic knowledge and skills as the route to decode words Spelling: words containing each of the 40+ phonemes already taught	Resources Whiteboards and markers Magnetic letters Phonics story and song TA to work with MA Teacher to work with LA. Word cards Word list on board
Revise Revise all the sounds taught so far using flashcards. The children say each sound once quickly with pure annunciation. If they have learnt actions for the sounds, they do not use them here as the object is quick recall; the actions are prompts when the children are reading or writing. Revise the letter sound (and action) from the previous day.		
Teach Show the children the digraph **oa**. Tell them that the letter o and a (use the letter names) together make the **oa** sound. Model saying the sound, then have the children say the sound. Teach them that "If two vowels go walking, the first one does the talking" we use the first vowels name as the sound. If there is an action, teach the children the action. Then read or tell a story containing the sound. The children show you the action or indicate when they hear the new sound. Watch the children and see who is hearing the sound and who is finding this task difficult. The children then tell you the words they heard in the story containing the sound. Some only hear words containing the initial sound, but others hear the sound in the middle or end of the word. Sing a song or say a rhyme containing the sound, preferably with actions.		
Supported Practice Show the children the **oa** digraph in words on the board, underline the digraph or write it in another colour so that children can see it clearly. Model sounding out and blending each word. The second time you segment and blend the word, read it with the children. The third time the children segment and blend the word independently, either individually or as a group. I use the phrases, 'My turn…Our turn…' and 'Your turn…' Teacher: My turn… **b-oa-t**, **boat** Teacher and children: Our turn…**b-oa-t**, **boat** Teacher: Your turn… Children: **b-oa-t**, **boat**		

Application

The children then have a go at writing or making a few words with the **oa** digraph. Cover up the words on the board or use new words; the children listen to the sounds and write the words; this is an opportunity to see who can hear the sounds and write the sounds they hear.

For each word, the children should:

Say the word

Count the sounds

Write the sounds to form a word

Check the word (The number of sounds, if the sounds are in order and if the word makes sense)

Lower Ability	Middle Ability	Higher Ability HA children can write the word in a sentence.
LA children can be given the word and then use letter manipulatives to make the word on top of the word card.	The teacher says a word, and the children sound out and make or write the word.	

Plenary

Recap what the sound looks like and the sound. Sort word cards into groups, words that contain the **oa** sound and those that do not.

Assessment

Use formative assessment and watch the children to see who can hear the sound, recognise the sound, and write the sound. Look out for children who write the sound the wrong way round or struggling to see digraphs in words.

Next Steps

Decide on the next steps based on the children's abilities.

Small-Group Phonics Intervention Teaching the or Sound		
Subject: English	Year group:1	Date:
Lesson Objectives To understand and remember how to read and write the **or** sound in words.	Curriculum Links English-Reading-Word reading: apply phonic knowledge and skills as the route to decode words Spelling: words containing each of the 40+ phonemes already taught.	Resources Whiteboards and markers Magnetic letters Word cards and a list

Revise

Revise all the sounds taught so far using flashcards. The children say each sound once quickly with pure annunciation. If they have learnt actions for the sounds, they do not use them here as the object is quick recall; the actions are prompts when the children are reading or writing.
Revise the letter sound (and action) from the previous day.

Teach

Show the children the sound. Model saying the sound, then have the children say the sound. If there is an action, teach the children the action. Play auditory games where you sound out a word, and the child guesses the word. Then reverse this and say a word and have the children sound it out.

Supported Practice

Show the children a word card and model sounding out the word, then blending the word. Then have the children sound out and blend the word. Continue with a few more words; for each word, the children must say the word, count the sounds, write the sounds, and then check the word.
Use the phrases, 'My turn…Our turn…' and 'Your turn…'
Teacher: My turn… **sh-or-t**, sh**ort**
Teacher and children: Our turn…**sh-or-t**, sh**ort**
Teacher: Your turn…
Children: **sh-or-t**, **short**

Application For each word, the teacher questions and guides the children:
The teacher shows the children the word **fort.**
What does this word say? Let's sound it out together **f-or-t**, **fort**, let's do that again, **f-or-t**, **fort**.
How many sounds are in the word **fort**?
Let's draw three sound buttons.
What is the first sound you can hear in the word **fort**?

Let's make that sound and place it on top of the first sound button. What is the second sound you can hear in the word **fort**? Let's make that sound and place it on top of the second sound button. What is the last sound you can hear in the word **fort**? Let's make the sound and place it on top of the last sound button. Let's read the word **f-or-t**, **fort**. Great now let's write the word. How many syllables are in the word **fort**? Do you know any words that rhyme with **fort**? Can you make a sentence with the word **fort**?
Plenary Recap what the sound looks like and the sounds. Read the **or** words made together.
Assessment Use formative assessment and watch the children to see who can hear the sound, recognise the sound, and write the sound. Look out for children who write the sound the wrong way round or struggling to see digraphs in words.
Next Steps Decide on the next steps based on the children's abilities.

A Writing Lesson Teaching the conjunction *and.*		
Subject: English	Year group:1	Date:
Lesson Objectives To use the joining word **and** to join ideas and sentences.	Curriculum Links English- To use the joining word **and** to link ideas and sentences.	Resources Whiteboards Picture cards
Revise How to write a sentence with a couple of short, dictated sentences on whiteboards: Think it (Think about what to write) Say it (Say the sentence, counting the words, this can be said more than once.) Write it (Write the sentence.) Check it (Check the sentence, for capital letters, full stops, finger spaces, the number of words in the sentence and to ensure it makes sense.)		
Teach Write a simple sentence in the board, then feign disappointment in what you have written, then come up with the idea of making the sentence more interesting. Tell the children that you are going to use the word **and** in the sentence to make the sentence more interesting. Then model using the word and by rewriting the sentence underneath the first sentence to show the improvement in the sentence.		
Supported Practice Have the children write a simple dictated sentence on their whiteboards. Then get some ideas from the class about how they could make the sentence better using the word and. Decide on the best idea and have all the children improve their sentence by rewriting the sentence using and. Repeat this process until you see a child rubbing out the full stop and using and with the new ending, then have the children rub out the full stop and complete their sentences using and the new ending to the sentence. Gradually increase the independence the children have by allowing them to come up with their own ideas. When you are confident most children can use the conjunction and in a sentence independently then move on to the application phase.		
Application Give the children some picture cards to choose from. The children pick a card, write a sentence in their books using the conjunction and then replace the card and choose another picture.		

Lower Ability	Middle Ability	Higher Ability
The children who struggled to write a sentence using **and** during the input should be grouped together and supported with the sentence writing by an adult.	Children pick pictures and write sentences using the conjunction **and**, they can ask for ideas and advice from their peers if they need support.	Once these children have written a few sentences correctly using the conjunction **and** they can be challenged to write sentences using the conjunction **because**.

Plenary

Pick a few children's books and show the class what they have done well on the visualiser. The children can also come up with next steps for the work that is shown such as capital letters, full stops, finger spaces, spelling, or neat handwriting. This helps children better evaluate their own learning.

Assessment

Formative assessment during the input and summative assessment of the work in the books.

Next Steps

Decide on the next steps based on the children's abilities.

A **Guided Reading Lesson to Develop Fluency**		
Subject: English	Year group:2	Date:
Lesson Objectives To read a sentence fluently.	Curriculum Links English- to read words accurately and fluently without overt sounding and blending.	Resources Common Exception Words List (ey words) Magnetic Letters Volcano Comprehension Short text comprehension Owl Babies Books
Group 1: Higher Ability-Independent Volcano Comprehension: Children read and answer questions on their own based on a non-fiction text about volcanoes. This text should be slightly challenging but easy enough for the children to work on independently		
Group 2: Middle Ability-Independent Children read and answer questions on a short text that has been pre-taught in a previous guided reading lesson.		
3: Group 3: Middle Ability- With teacher Text: Owl Babies **Revise** 1: Revise this week's common exception words with flashcards (key, money, honey, alley) **Teach** Look at new vocabulary in the book, read the words on word cards and discuss their meaning. **Supported Practice** Each child in the group and the teacher takes turns to read a page in the book. With the teacher supporting the children with their sounding out and blending. **Application** Once the book is complete the children pick their favourite page and practice reading a sentence on that page for a few minutes. They then read that sentence through once. Explain to the children that they are going to reread the sentence several times to develop greater fluency. Demonstrate what good fluency sounds like. Now have the child read the first word of the sentence while you cover the rest of the sentence. They then read the first and second word, then the first, second, third word and then the first, second, third and fourth word until the sentence is complete. They should have greater fluency by the end of the sentence. Then move on to the next child. While one child is reading their sentence, the others can be practising theirs quietly in their heads. **Plenary** Have each child read their sentence to the group to demonstrate reading with fluency.		

Group 4: Lower Ability- With Teaching Assistant
Text: Volcanoes: Non-fiction text
Revise
1: Revise this week's common exception words with flashcards (key, money, honey, alley)
Teach
Look at new vocabulary in the text, read the words on word cards and discuss their meaning.
Supported Practice
Read the text together as a group, then re-read the text, with each child reading a few sentences independently.
Application
Look at and discussing questions and where to find the answers.
Plenary
Discuss the text; what do they know about volcanoes, what would they like to find out, would they like to see one?

Group 5: SEND-Independent
Children read Common Exception Words (on the list provided) and make the words using magnetic letters on top of the words.

Assessment
Formative assessment of children's reading ability based on Year Two reading criteria. Summative assessment of the completed reading comprehensions for groups 1 and 2.

Next Steps
Decide on the next steps based on the children's abilities.

<table>
<tr><td colspan="3">A Reading Comprehension Lesson to teach how to find the Answers</td></tr>
<tr><td>Subject: English</td><td>Year group:2</td><td>Date:</td></tr>
<tr><td>Lesson Objectives
To read a story and answer questions about the story.</td><td>Curriculum Links
English- T read a text and answer questions, making some inferences (HA: on a text read independently).</td><td>Resources
3 texts on 3 different reading ability levels.</td></tr>
<tr><td colspan="3">Revise
Talk about how to read a text. Using a bookmark or finger to keep our place and thinking about what we are reading.</td></tr>
<tr><td colspan="3">Teach
Place the text on the smartboard and cover all the text except the line you are reading to resemble using a bookmark. Model reading the text. Then read the first question and underline the NB information in the sentence, then model finding the answer in the text, underlining the answer, and writing the answer.</td></tr>
<tr><td colspan="3">Supported Practice
Continue with a few more questions letting the children help you find and write the answers to the questions. No more than three questions with one of them being an inference question.</td></tr>
<tr><td colspan="3">Application
The children now answer comprehensions on a text that is on their reading level using the technique taught on the board.</td></tr>
<tr><td>Lower Ability
These children answer the same text that was modelled on the board as well as the same questions, they may ask each other for help.</td><td>Middle Ability
These 2 groups work with an adult, (the TA and the teacher). They work through a comprehension with the adult, the adult reminds them of the technique taught and assesses the children throughout the process.</td><td>Higher Ability
These children read an unseen text on their own and answer the questions.</td></tr>
<tr><td colspan="3">Plenary
Pick one or two children to show their work and explain to the class how they found the answers to the comprehension questions. Pick a LA, MA, and HA child.</td></tr>
<tr><td colspan="3">Assessment
Formative assessment during the input and application phase. Summative assessment of the LA and HA comprehension answers.</td></tr>
<tr><td colspan="3">Next Steps
Decide on the next steps based on the children's abilities.</td></tr>
</table>

A **Spelling Lesson**		
Subject: English	Year group:2	Date:
Lesson Objectives To spell words with the j sound spelt as **g** and **dge.**	**Curriculum Links** English- To spell phonemes with alternate graphemes.	**Resources** Word list Tricky Train Chart White board markers Magnetic letters

Revise

Use flashcards to revise previously learnt phonemes and graphemes. Pick one or two words from the word lists on the back of the flashcards for children to spell.

Teach

Show the children the two new graphemes (ge and dge) for the phoneme j.
Teach the children the spelling the rules and write them on the board as a reference:
We use **g** for the **j** sound when the sound comes before the letters **e, i** or **y**.
We use **dge** for the **j** sound at the end of a word when the vowel sound is short.

Supported Practice

On the smart board slowly work through the word badge on the Tricky Train board with the children working on their boards at the same time.
Write the word **badge** in the speech bubble and have them copy the word. The children say the word; if they cannot read the word, then tell them what the word is; they then repeat it.
The children count the sounds **b-a-dge**, and colour in three sound clouds.
The children (LA) make the word using letter manipulatives and place them over the cloud sound buttons.
The children write the sounds into the train carts, one sound per cart.

b	a	dge

The children write the irregular sound on the train track as a rock **dge**.
Go through the elements on the train ticket: the children identify and says the first: **b**, middle **a** and last sound **dge**. They say any words that rhyme with the word. They count and clap the syllables (1) and identify any blends(none).
The children draw a picture for the word into the magnifying glass.
The children write the word on the line using dots and dashes under the graphemes to denote graphs, digraphs and trigraphs and

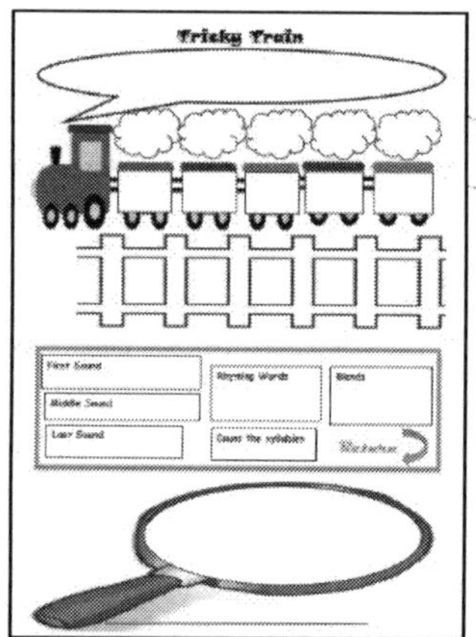

spell it out loud using the letter names. Any digraghs and trigraphs are spelled out quicker to help with retention.

Application:
The children then use their Tricky Trains to learn the rest of the words in their spelling list.

Lower Ability	**Middle Ability**	**Higher Ability**
These children use letter manipulatives as well as the other activities to complete each word on the Tricky Train chart. They work with an adult.	These children use their Tricky Train charts to learn the words on their spelling lists, they are supported by their peers and an adult if one is available.	These children complete the spelling words on their Tricky Train Charts then write sentences in their books using the words on their spelling list.

Plenary
The children play a spelling game where they try to write the spelling word faster than the teacher. They spell one or two of the words they have learnt on their whiteboards but with the addition of prefixes or suffixes.

Assessment
Formative assessment during the lesson. Summative assessment at the end of the week based on the spelling test.

Next Steps	**Word List**	**Extension list**
Decide on the next steps based on the outcome of the lesson and the spelling test. Reteach any words that most of the children struggled with and retest these words at a later stage. The children also practice any words they got wrong in the spelling test. LA children may only write a test on a few of the words. .	badge bridge fudge orange jam joke gem magic	badges bridges bridged oranges gems joking joked magically magician

A **Grammar Lesson Teaching Verbs**

Subject: English	Year group:2	Date:
Lesson Objectives To identify verbs in a sentence	**Curriculum Links** English- To understand the term verb and identify and use verbs in a sentence.	**Resources** Nessy video on You Tube Flow chart Word list Sentence worksheet

Revise
Remind the children of nouns and adjectives

Teach
Tell the children they are going to learn about a new group of words called verbs. Verbs are doing words; they are the words in the sentence which tell us what is happening. Watch the Nessy clip on YouTube: Amazing Newt Vibrating.

Supported Practice
The children divide their whiteboards into three columns with the heading's adjective, noun, and verb. They then work through a few words with the teacher to place the words in the right columns using the flow chart on the board to help them categorise the words.

Application
Once the children understand the difference between the words. Then give them a sentence where they need to find the verb, circle the word, and label it: verb. Labelling the word will reinforce the learning. They find the verb by asking themselves the question: "What are they **doing** in this sentence?"

Lower Ability	**Middle Ability**	**Higher Ability**
These children are supported by an adult reminding them of the question: What are they doing?	The question is written on a card to help them work independently.	These children need to find and label the verb, adjective, and noun in each sentence.

Plenary
Each child writes their own sentence on a whiteboard including a noun, verb and adjective and label the words.

Assessment
Formative assessment during the input and while working with the LA. Summative assessment of the independent work produced by the MA and HA.

Next Steps
Decide on the next steps based on the children's abilities.

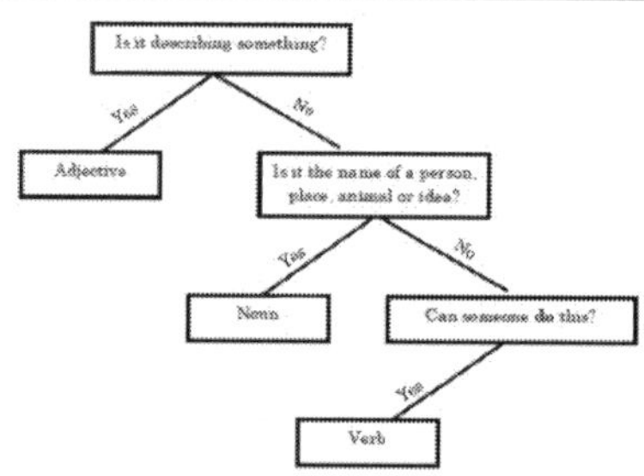

13 PRE-READING, WRITING AND SPELLING ACTIVITIES

Visual Perception

Visual perception is the child's ability to make sense of what they see; a child can have perfect vision but still struggle with visual perception. Most activities to develop visual perception will occur in Nursery and Reception, but children struggling with these skills need to continue these activities in Year One and Two.

Teaching Left to Right

For children that struggle to remember to read/write from left to right, place a green sticker on the left-hand side of the text or page to remind them where to start and a red sticker on the right of the page to show them where to stop. Use the mantra: "We read from left to right and top to bottom" at the beginning of every reading and writing lesson until the children do this naturally.

Puzzles

Puzzles can be challenging for children who struggle with visual perception. Start with simple puzzles and build up to more challenging puzzles with more pieces. Some children do not know how to build a puzzle and you will need to teach these children how to make a puzzle.

1. Use the picture on the box as a reference.
2. Look for the corner pieces and put them in place.
3. Look for all the straight pieces and build the outside.
4. Look for pieces with the same colours, textures, and shapes to complete the puzzle.
5. If the puzzle piece will only go in when you force it, then it is the wring piece.

Bookmarks

To develop visual tracking skills children should use their finger or a bookmark to keep their place when reading. This helps train the eyes to move from left to right and focus on the word or sentence rather than bounce around the page.

Wooden Pattern Blocks

Wooden pattern blocks help children with a range of visual skills. These consist of 2D wooden shapes and picture instruction cards made from shapes. The child then uses the wooden blocks to copy the instruction cards. You can make your own or buy them in sets with activity cards for the child to copy. Children will find these tasks particularly challenging at first and will need support.

Construction Games

Construction games such as Lego, Duplo, Knex, Magnetic Building Blocks, Meccano and wooden blocks help children develop spatial awareness. They also enhance fine motor skills and creativity.

Dot-to-Dots

Dot-to-dots are pictures created when the child connects the dots, these dots are normally numbered, and the child draws a line from the first number to the last number chronologically. Start the child on simple dot-to-dots and then build up to more complicated pictures. Pictures that look easy to an adult can be overwhelming to a child. Dot-to-dots develop fine motor control, visual figure-ground and visual spatial relations skills.

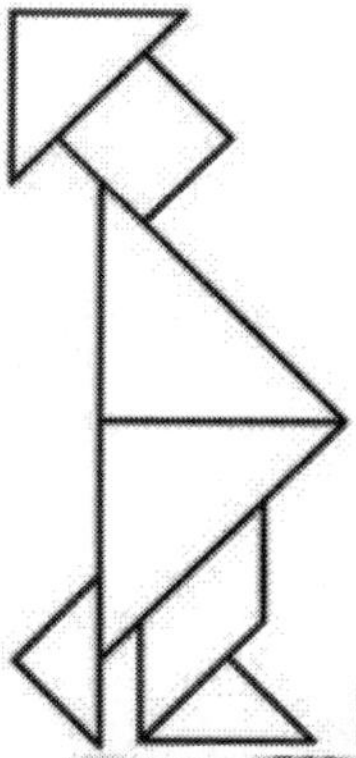

Tangrams

Tangrams are ancient Chinese geometrical puzzles that consist of a square cut into seven shapes. The shapes are rearranged to create pictures. The most accessible tangram puzzles show where each puzzle piece belongs in the picture, and the most challenging puzzles present the picture as a silhouette. Tangrams develop visual discrimination, spatial relations, figure-ground, sequential memory, and form constancy skills.

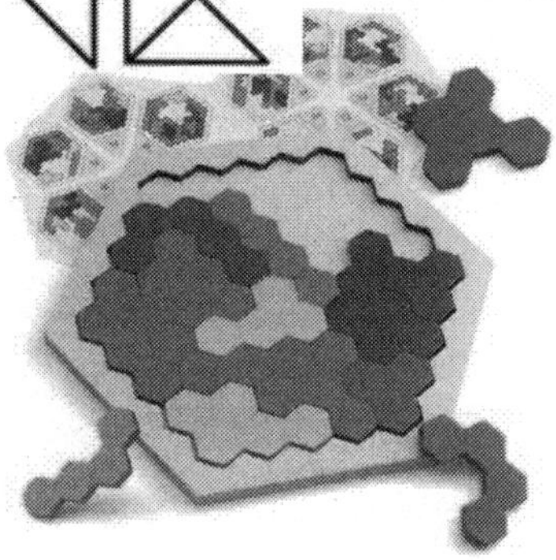

Coogam Wooden Shape Puzzles

Coogam makes a variety of different shape puzzles. The puzzles normally consist of shapes fitted into a wooden base board. The children then copy picture instruction cards to complete the puzzle. The activity cards range in complexity and suit any age. Children can do these activities independently or in small groups. These puzzles develop fine motor control, visual closure, visual discrimination, visual figure ground and visual spatial relations skills.

An Eye Spy Buddy

Make an Eye Spy Buddy by gluing a googly eye onto a lolly stick. The children use the stick to point at each word as they read. They can also use the Eye Spy Buddy to make finger spaces between words when writing sentences. An Eye Spy Buddy helps the child develop visual tracking skills as well as fluency.

Mosaic Block Pictures

A Mosaic block game is where square tiles are placed on a grid to reproduce a picture instruction card. Coogam makes a lovely wooden Mosaic Block Game that will last a long time even in a busy classroom. Children love copying patterns onto the mosaic board. They can also make up patterns or designs, copy a friend's or make words or shapes with the tiles. Mosaic Block Pictures develop fine motor, visual discrimination, visual figure-ground and visual spatial relations skills as well as creativity and problem solving.

Dobble

Dobble is a card game played with round cards; each card has several pictures of objects printed on them. The cards are shared out between two or three children. The children hold the cards face down and then take turns placing cards face up on a stack in the centre of the table. If a child places a matching card on the pile, they quickly put their hand on the set and says the name of the matching item. The first one to place their hand down gets all the cards. The game is won when one child has the whole stack. Dobble develops visual discrimination, form constancy, figure-ground, and vocabulary skills.

Snap

Sets of snap cards are available everywhere. Share out the cards between two or three players. The children hold their cards face down and when it is their turn, they place a card face up on the stack on the table. When two consecutive cards are the same, the child says "Snap" while placing their hand on the stack. The first child to say "Snap" gets the stack. The game is won when one child has the whole pile. This game is good for visual discrimination and visual memory skills.

Q-bitz

Q-Bitz is a 3D puzzle game. The instruction card is placed on the table, and all the players replicate the card as fast as possible. The card can also be shown and then turned over, working on the child's memory skills. This game develops visual discrimination, form constancy, figure-ground discrimination, and visual closure skills.

Complete the Picture

Children are given a picture with parts of the image missing. They then draw to complete the picture. If children are new to this activity, then start with small areas of the picture missing and work up to pictures where half the image is removed. Symmetrical pictures are good for these types of activities. Complete the picture activities develop figure-ground, visual closure and spatial relations and problem-solving skills.

Hidden Picture Activities

Give the child a page filled with lots of small images; children's mindfulness colouring books are an excellent place to find these. The child can then look for specific items and colour or circle them when they find them. Hidden picture activities develop visual discrimination, visual figure-ground and visual attention.

Hidden Picture Books

Hidden picture books like the *Where's Wally* books are great fun and develop visual discrimination, visual figure-ground and visual attention skills. These books can be used on a one-to-one basis, in small groups, or freely available to children in the book corner.

I Spy

Play I spy with the children. There are many variations of this game. Play with a game board, an I Spy Book or an I Spy Bottle filled with rice and small toys. When children are still learning to read and write, use the letter sound and not the letter name. I Spy develops a child's visual discrimination, form constancy, visual memory, and figure-ground skills.

Kim's Game

Kim's game is a visual memory game. Place a few objects on a tray. The child looks at the items and tries to memorise them. Then you cover the objects and have the child say what was on the table. Alternatively, cover the objects and remove one object and see if the child can identify what is missing when the things are uncovered. Start with three or four objects and build to more over time.

Pom-Pom Patterns

Create pom-pom pattern instruction cards by arranging coloured circles on a line. These cards can be made on the computer or simple stick circular stickers in a row on a strip of paper. Give the child the instruction card and they place the pom poms in order according to the card. This develops visual discrimination and visual sequential memory.

Heads and Tails Puzzles

Heads and tails puzzles are pictures where the children need to match half an animal or person with the other half. These puzzles can be bought, or you can make them by cutting images in half. These puzzles develop visual attention, visual discrimination, and visual spatial relations skills. Older children can write a list of the animals they make or write sentences about the animals.

Spot the Difference

Children compare pictures to find the differences. Start with simple images with obvious differences; this is a good activity for children with visual discrimination difficulties.

Egg Carton Patterns

Cheap plastic eggs are available everywhere at Easter time. Make simple egg pattern instruction cards using an array of coloured ovals. The children copy the instruction cards and put plastic eggs into egg cartons. Some children may struggle to do this activity due to colour blindness. This activity develops visual discrimination and visual spatial relations skills.

Blink

Blink is a card game that can be played with a small group of children. It is like Snap, except the pictures can be matched by the symbol, the number of objects or colour. This game is suitable for visual form constancy and visual discrimination skills.

Mental Blox

Mental Blox is a puzzle game that can be played independently or in a small group. There are picture instruction cards; the children reproduce the images on the cards using the blocks. Mental Blox is excellent for visual discrimination spatial relations, visual closure, and form constancy.

Sorting Bear Patterns

Make or download sorting bear instruction cards. The children then create the patterns using counting bears. Twinkl has Sorting bear instruction cards. This activity can be tricky for children who are colour blind. It develops visual sequency, visual memory, and visual spatial relations skills.

Peg Boards

Teach children how to copy a pegboard pattern. Show them how to work from top to bottom and left to right. Pegboard patterns develop spatial relation and visual closure skills.

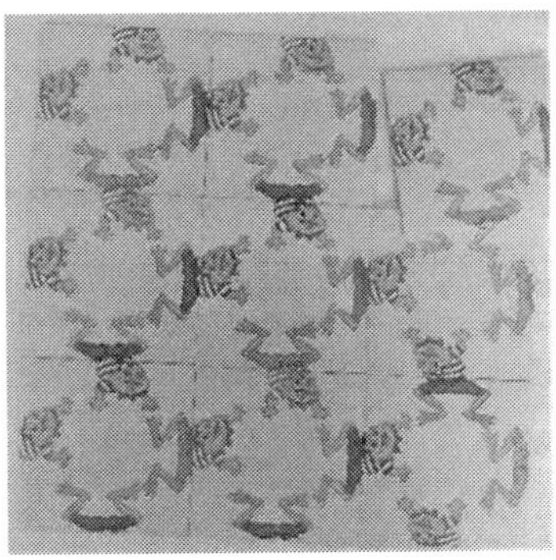

Scramble Squares

Scramble squares are puzzles created with nine identically sized squares. On each side is the top or bottom of an animal or person with small differences. The squares are then arranged so that all the sides match up. They require children to pay careful attention to visual details in the pictures to solve the puzzle and give no self-correcting cues. Older children love these puzzles; however, children with visual difficulties will find these frustrating and need support. These puzzles are particularly good for developing visual attention, visual discrimination, and visual figure-ground skills.

Lollipop Pictures

Create shapes and pictures using coloured lollipop sticks and then photograph them to create instruction cards. The child then copies the instruction cards using lollipop sticks. *Twinkl* has ready-made lollipop instruction cards available for printing. This develops visual spatial relations skills.

Lego Patterns

Create or photograph Lego pattern cards with brick towers of different coloured bricks and shape cards where the bricks create different shapes. The children then copy the patterns using Lego. Twinkl has ready-made Lego instruction cards available to download. This activity can be tricky for children who are colour blind. This activity develops fine motor. visual sequency, visual spatial relations predicting and problem-solving skills.

Shape Pattern Cards

Create a set of shapes and a set of shape instruction cards. The child then copies the instruction cards using the shapes. This activity can be tricky for children who are colour blind. This activity develops visual sequency, visual memory, visual discrimination, and visual spatial relations skills.

Caterpillar Patterns

Create or download caterpillar instruction cards. The child then copies the caterpillar card pattern by sticking circle stickers onto paper. Alternatively, they could replicate the pattern using pom poms. This activity can be tricky for children who are colour blind. This activity develops visual sequency and visual discrimination.

Geoboards

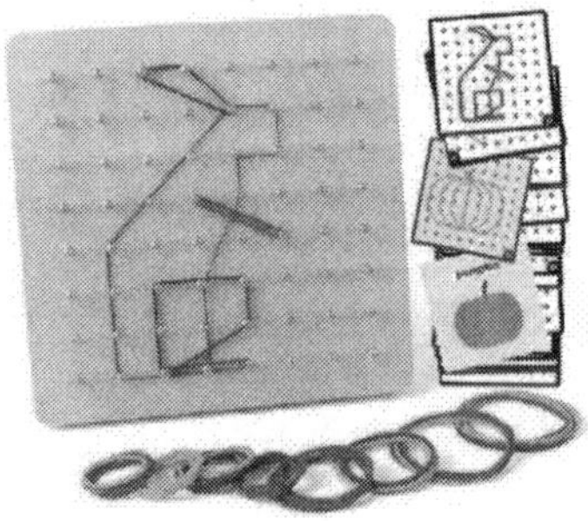

Geoboards are boards that have pegs or nails on with elastic bands stretched over the pegs to create the pictures. You can download geoboard instruction cards, or you can create a pattern card by photographing elastic pictures on a geoboard. The child copies the instruction card by stretching coloured elastic bands around pegs on a board. This activity can be tricky for children who are colour blind. This activity develops children's visual perceptual skills and fine motor skills at the same time.

Picture Dominoes

Give each child five picture dominoes and place the rest upside down on the table. The first child puts down a domino on the table. The next child puts down a matching picture domino touching the one on the table. If they have no matching pictures, they take a domino from the pile. If they can use the new domino, they do, or they pass, and it is the next child's turn. The first player to use all their dominoes is the winner. Picture dominoes develops visual discrimination. Children can play with traditional number dot dominoes as well.

Lite-Brite

Lite-Brite works on the same concept as a pegboard. Children copy pattern cards to create a picture using pegs on a board. When they are finished, they can turn on the light, and their work is brought to life using lights. The lights adds an element of reward to this game that children enjoy. Lite-Brite develops visual closure and spatial relations.

Numicon Pattern Boards

Numicon pattern cards fit onto the Numicon baseboards. The child then uses the Numicon pieces to make the picture. The picture cards can also be placed on the table for the child to copy. Alternatively, the child can copy a pattern created by the teacher or another child. This activity develops visual discrimination, visual figure-ground, and visual spatial relations skills.

Rush Hour

Rush Hour is a traffic jam grid game where the child sets up their game in the same way as the instruction card by sliding their pieces on the grid. It comes with challenge cards on various levels and is an excellent game for a range of ages. It is a good activity for children with visual discrimination and spatial relation difficulties and children with processing and planning challenges.

Memory Game

Children love playing Memory Game. Buy these games ready-made or make your own by printing a set of cards with pairs of matching pictures. Place the cards face down on the table. The children take turns to uncover two cards; if the cards match, they can keep the cards and have another go; if they do not, they turn the cards back over, and it is the next child's turn. Memory Game develops visual discrimination, form constancy and visual memory skills.

Simon

The children can play Simon in small groups, or independently. The child watches a sequence of coloured lights and then repeats the sequence. This activity can be tricky for children who are colour blind. This is a great game to develop visual sequential memory and discrimination.

Fine Motor Skills

Gross motor control is the overall control of the whole body, posture, balance, and limb control. Fine motor control is power over the small muscles and the hands and fingers. Children need control over both their gross and fine motor muscles before learning to write. Here are a few ideas to develop handwriting and fine motor control. Children need to play and be active, provide plenty of opportunities for children to move.

Play Trail

Children should be encouraged to play outdoors and to climb on and use the play trail. Monkey bars and firemen's poles are good for shoulder stability.

Skipping Ropes

Skipping can be an incredibly challenging skill for some children. Children who master skipping at a young age will have better core strength and shoulder stability and be better prepared for writing.

Bean Bags and Balls

Encourage catching and throwing activities. Have the child pass objects across their bodies. They should use both hands, one hand and swap hands when playing with balls and beanbags.

Jenga

Jenga is a great small group game. The children stack the blocks and then remove the blocks one at a time without toppling the tower. This game also develops concentration.

Ribbon Sticks

Children play with ribbons attached to dowelling sticks to make large movements. They draw patterns and letters in the air using their ribbon wands. They make swirling, sliding, hopping, jumping movements with their wands and move fast and slowly. Encourage children to swap hands and to use two hands. Let the children dance to music with their ribbon sticks.

Weaving

Children weave ribbons, leaves, or flowers through metal weaving frames. If there are no weaving frames available, they can weave ribbons through the school fence or an old bicycle wheel.

Stress Balls

Make a flour friend with the child using corn starch and a balloon. You can then draw a face on the friend. The child squeezes and manipulates their friend while developing strength.

Bread Making

Make bread dough with the children. The children then knead and manipulate the dough to shape the bread. Add chocolate chips, cinnamon, and raisins or to the bread dough to make it more interesting.

Biscuit Baking

Make a simple biscuit dough mixture. The child kneads the dough, spoons it out and rolls it into balls. They can make fork patterns on the dough when they are finished. They love taking these home to show their parents.

Yoga Ball

The child sits on a yoga ball to develop core strength or plays with a space hopper. This is an excellent idea for home as well as the child can create balance and core strength while watching television, drawing, or eating.

Brain Gym

Brain Gym is a programme of short physical activities that develop the skills needed for the body to work and learn effectively. They recall the movements that are natural in the child's first few years of life. The teacher uses a book to do Brain Gym exercises, completes a course, or becomes a facilitator.

Pasta or Cereal Necklaces

Children thread pasta or cereal onto string to make necklaces. You can buy ready dyed pasta, or the children can paint their jewellery.

Stone Patterns

Print some large patterns on card. The child then places pebbles, gems, or other items on the patterns.

Two-Handed Writing

Give the children two chunky crayons and have them place one in each hand. They then draw/doodle/scribble using both hands simultaneously; this can be on paper on a table, floor, or a standing easel.

Threading

Cut around a picture printed on a firm card. Punch holes around the edge; the children then thread around the images. You can also cut around cereal box pictures or buy ready-made threading cards or blocks.

Beads

Children thread beads onto pipe cleaners to make bangles. Twist the first bead onto the pipe cleaner so that the beads do not slip off then twist the pipe cleaner to secure the bangle.

Playdoh

Show the children how to roll the dough into balls or sausages and use cookie cutters. Let them use plastic knives, forks, spoons, and playdoh punches in their play. Encourage them to squeeze and shape the dough in their hands.

Therapy Putty

Therapy Putty is used in a similar way to a stress ball. It is squeezed and manipulated in the hand and gives the child excellent sensory feedback. It comes in different resistances so the child can build up their fine motor strength.

Cutting Activities

The child should be encouraged to cut often. At first, the child will need adult assistance; they will then begin snipping and will later use cutting strokes to cut objects. Provide paper, leaves, card, tissue, and material for the child to cut.

Tongs

Children love playing with tongs or large tweezers. Give them a challenge, such as moving the pom-poms into a bowl.

Write Dance

Write Dance is a programme specifically developed to use music and play to develop young children's fine motor skills. Do Write Dance with the whole class or with smaller groups.

Beaded Trees

Place some sticks in playdoh or salt dough so that the sticks stand up like mini trees. The children then thread on pony beads to decorate the trees. This activity can double as an Easter or Christmas craft.

Craft

Provide lots of opportunities for craft. These can be structured or free play activities. Put out paint, glitter, stickers, different types of scissors, card, material, felt and felt tips. The children will love opportunities to be creative.

Junk Modelling

Collect recycling such as egg boxes, cereal boxes, paper towel tubes and lids and allow the children to use them to create their models. Junk modelling requires children to engage in different fine motor activities for extended periods and use their imagination.

Save The Animals

Cover small world animals in elastic bands. The child then "frees" the animals from the elastics. Children love this activity.

Pinecone Elastics

Put out a tub of pinecones and elastic bands. The children then cover the pinecones in elastic bands. Reverse this activity and have the children remove the elastic bands from the pinecones.

Tennis Ball Monsters

Cut a slit into a tennis ball and stick some eyes onto the tennis ball. The child feeds the tennis ball small objects by squeezing the tennis ball to open the monster's mouth.

Phonological Awareness

Phonological awareness is the understanding that words are made from sounds and sentences are made from words. Phonological activities can be done with your eyes closed; they are all about what you can hear.

Nursery Rhymes

Sing Nursery Rhymes, songs, and chants with the children. Include lots of body percussion and actions. Songs with rhyme and alliteration develop an understanding of the similarities and differences in words. They develop speech patterns, intonation, cadence, and auditory memory and sequencing.

Mirror Mirror

Each child has a mirror, and they make noises while looking in the mirror or they pull faces and imitate the sounds and actions the teacher makes while looking in the mirror. Such as puffing out your cheeks and blowing bubbles like a fish, pulling a tongue, or chirping like a bird. This game develops auditory memory and auditory discrimination.

Vocal Noises

Use sound words and have the children copy you. These can be action words, animal noises or any other sound words. For example, you can moo like a cow or swing up high, whee or bounce the ball, boing, boing, boing or be quiet like a mouse, shshsh. This activity develops auditory memory and auditory discrimination.

Sound Ping Pong

Play sound call and repeat games with the children. You make a sound, and the children echo the sound back for example you can say, "Ee-or, ee-or" and the children copy you saying "Ee-or, ee-or." Or you could say, "Wheee-bump!" and the children repeat, "Wheee-bump!" This game develops auditory memory and auditory discrimination.

Farm or Zoo Animal Small World

Provide farm or zoo animal small world toys for the children to use during free play. Encourage them to make animal noises as part of their play. This activity develops auditory discrimination.

Animal Masks

Give the children animal masks to use for role play. Ask the children what noises the different animals make and encourage them to imitate the animals. This activity develops auditory discrimination.

Musical Statues

All the children dance freely. When the music stops, they freeze, and when the music starts, they can dance again; this is also a great movement break. This game develops auditory attention and auditory figure ground discrimination.

Sound Stories

Read the children stories with lots of sounds where the children can join in with the sound effects like *Hairy McClary from Donaldson's Dairy* or What the Ladybird Heard by Julia Donaldson. This activity develops auditory memory and auditory discrimination.

Mystery Sounds

Record sounds around the house or school on a tablet. Then play the sounds to the children, and the children guess what the sounds are; this can be a regular game, and the child that guesses correctly could be named the Super Sound Detective for the day. Children love fun titles. This game develops auditory figure-ground discrimination and auditory discrimination.

Secret Sounds

Use opaque bottles, tins, or boxes, half fill them with different ingredients making sure each bottle has a pair. You can use popcorn kernels, beans, rice, sand, water, Lego, beads, or any other small object that would make a distinct sound when the bottle is shaken as fillers. The children then shake each bottle and find its pair. This game develops auditory discrimination and auditory figure-ground discrimination.

Water Xylophone

Put several identical glass jars on the table. Fill the first with water and then put slightly less water in each subsequent jar. The children then use a teaspoon to play the water xylophone. Closely monitor this activity for safety reasons. This activity develops auditory figure-ground discrimination and auditory discrimination.

Bottle Top Castanets

Glue two bottle tops on a piece of card, then fold the card over so that the tops can clap together to create a castanet. The children then create or copy musical beats using their castanets. Musical instruments develop auditory discrimination.

Musical Chairs

Play musical chairs a small group of children as it is a difficult game to manage with lots of children. Place chairs in the middle of the room, using one less chair than the number of children. Put on the music and let the children dance freely. When the music stops, they must find a chair and sit down quickly. The child without a chair stands out. You can then remove a chair and play again until one chair is left in the centre and the child sitting on it is the winner. This game develops auditory figure-ground discrimination and auditory discrimination.

Rhythm Games

Clap out a beat and have children move around the area in time with the rhythm. Children love to pretend so have them be characters while doing this activity, they could march like a soldier, hop like a bunny, or skip like a princess in time to the music. This game could also be played using a drum or a tambourine. These games develop auditory discrimination.

Clap and Repeat

The teacher claps a rhythm, and the children copy the pattern. The teacher can clap loudly, softly, fast, slow and vary the rhythm. This activity develops auditory memory and auditory sequencing.

Broken Down Telephone

Play this game in small groups as children lose focus when the group is too big. Whisper a sentence into the first child's ear, the child repeats what they heard to the second child and so on down then line. The last child then tells the group what they think the sentence is, and you can tell them the actual sentence. At first, some children find this game disconcerting because they feel they are getting something wrong when they hear a mixed-up sentence, but with a little repetition they will understand and enjoy the game more. This game develops auditory discrimination.

List Games

Start the game with a phrase and then fill in a noun. The next child repeats the phrase and your noun and adds a word of their own. Each subsequent child repeats the list and adds their word to the list. Once children know their alphabet each noun can be added in alphabetical order. This game develops auditory memory and auditory sequencing skills and is a great vocabulary builder.

A few sentence starters you could use are:

I went to the beach, and I saw…

I went to the park, and I heard…

I went to the ice cream shop, and I tasted…

I went to the market, and I smelt…

I went to school, and I felt…

Listening Pictures

Give the children a picture and have them colour it according to your instructions. Alternatively, you could give instructions, while the children draw their pictures. This activity develops auditory discrimination.

Talking Tins

Some children struggle with auditory memory; they find remembering a sentence long enough to write it down difficult. Give these children talking tin or another recording device; they record their sentence and then replay it to themselves to help them remember their sentence to write it down.

..

14 EARLY READING, WRITING AND SPELLING ACTIVITIES

Awareness of Words and Syllables

A child becomes aware of words when they start actively listening to and for words and playing with those words. They become aware of syllables when they can hear, clap or march to the rhythm or beat of words. Help children to hear and identify words in sentences with these games, hearing syllables becomes important when children start using more complex spelling rules in Year Two. **March The Words**

Say a sentence to the children, then repeat it while they march or clap to the beat of the sentence. Use one-syllable words for this activity as you are trying to demarcate words in a sentence. If you use two or three syllable words, it becomes harder for the children to hear the words as the syllables will insert extra beats into the sentence. Use the caption and sentence lists at the back of the book.

Count the Words

Say a sentence, then have the children repeat it while counting the words on their fingers. This activity is about saying the sentence and counting the words there is no writing at this point, you are trying to help children identify individual words and understand the concept of a word. Use the caption and sentence lists at the back of the book.

Pass the Clap

The children sit in a circle with their hands out at their sides. Each child's right hand is behind the child's left hand that is sitting on the right of them in the circle. The teacher starts the clap and passes it to the student on her right; the clap then goes around the circle. Once children are comfortable passing the clap, you can then introduce a sentence. The idea of this game is that there is one word for each clap.

Picture Cards

Print a set of simple pictures and words. Show the children the picture while covering the word. The children then say what the picture is, "tree." Then show the children the word; this builds an association between words and their meanings. The child is not reading the word; they are connecting the word with the image.

Hammer the Words

Say a sentence, and the child hammers in toy pegs while repeating the sentence. The child then counts the words based on the number of pegs hammered in.

Name Clapping

Name clapping is excellent for demonstrating syllables. Go around the class, helping the children clap out the rhythm of their names. Children find this tricky to begin with, but with time, they will clap out any word independently

Rhyming Words

Words that sound the same at the end are called rhyming words, they are also sometimes referred to as word families. Rhyming words are essential as children learn to listen for similarities and differences at the end of the words. Later, when children start learning to spell, word families make it easier for them to learn large groups of words instead of lots of words individually.

Do They Rhyme?

Explain to the children that rhyming words sound the same at the end of the word. Demonstrate these by saying a few rhyming words. Then play a game with the children, say two words, the children nod if the words rhyme and shake their heads if they do not.

Teacher: **cat/dog**

Children: 

Teacher: **cat/rat**

Children: 

Rhyming Pictures

Create cards with three pictures on them. The child then says what the three objects are and which two rhyme. They can then cross out the rhyming words or cover them with counters. Once children understand how to do this activity, they can then do it independently or in a small group.

Rhyming Tag

The teacher says a word; then the next child says a rhyming word until none of the children can think of another word. Then the game starts again with another word.

Teacher: **cat**
Child 1: **mat**
Child 2: **rat**
Child 3: **fat**

Rhyming Basket

Fill a basket with pairs of objects or pictures of things that rhyme. The children then take turns to find and say the rhyming pairs. This activity can be with an adult or in a small group.

Rhyming Books

Read rhyming picture books to the children and point out the rhyming words or over emphasise the words and try to get the children to notice them on their own. You could also have the children predict the rhyming pairs in the story; "I wonder what will rhyme with fox?"

Rhyming Bingo

Make or buy a Rhyming Bingo set with pictures of things that rhyme. The caller picks a picture card from a stack on the table and says the word for the image. Anyone with a picture that rhymes with the card can cover their picture. Each child gets a chance to be the caller. When a child covers their entire Bingo board, they call out Bingo and win the game. The children can then swop boards and play again.

What Rhymes With?

Give the children a target picture and a set of other pictures; some of the picture's rhyme with the target picture, and some do not. They say the names of the objects and decide which words rhyme with the target picture. This game is great for small group work and teach the children collaborative skills.

Rhyming I Spy

Play I Spy using rhyming words instead of sounds. Place some objects on a table and then have the children guess the word based on a rhyming word. I Spy can also be played with an I Spy picture board, or I Spy bottles.

Teacher: I Spy with my little eye something that rhymes with **dish**.

Children: **fish**!

Rhyming Pairs

Create picture cards of rhyming words. The children then sort these pictures into rhyming pairs. When children start learning to read you can add the words onto the cards. They are still however listening for the rhyming words and not necessarily reading the words, they are simply associating the words with the picture and building a greater understanding of the concept of words. Remember the aim of this activity is listening to and identifying rhyming words based on what they sound like, not look like.

Rhyming Memory Game

Create a set of rhyming word cards using only the graphemes taught so far. Each word should only have one possible match in the set and use the same ending graphemes to avoid confusion. Place all the word cards upside down on the table. Each child turns over two cards during their turn and reads the cards. If the cards are rhyming words, then they can keep the pair and have another turn. If not, they turn both cards back over, and the next child has a turn.

Rhyming Alphabet

Say a word then show the children how to go through the alphabet to find as many different rhyming words as possible by changing the initial sound. Be careful with this activity, I have made the mistake of not checking the alphabet rhyming words before and had a few inappropriate answers shouted at me across the classroom amid the child's excitement of discovering rhyming words. Never, ever, ever ask what rhymes with duck-don't say I didn't warn you…

Initial Sounds

The initial sound is the first sounds you can hear in word. They are also the easiest sounds for most children to hear; however, some children drop the initial sound when they first start writing as they forget the sound. When you are helping a child spell a word say the initial sound louder than the other sounds as this will help them remember the sound.

Object Sound Game

Place small world items or pictures beginning with the sounds the children have learnt in a basket. The child picks an object out of the basket, says the object's name and the initial sound. This activity can be extended by placing the sound cards on the table and the children can match the item to the sound.

Sound Book

Children keep a sound scrapbook. The teacher (or child) writes the grapheme on the page, and the children find and stick or write words containing the sound. They decorate each page with drawings, photographs, or pictures of objects containing the sound. Sound books are a fantastic Home Learning activity.

Picture Sound Game

Print a set of pictures of things beginning with the sounds the children have learnt. Place all the pictures face up on the table. Each child has a turn to say what the image is and the initial sound. When children are confident playing this game, you can place all the pictures face down and play again.

Initial Sound Odd One Out

Give the child three or four pictures. One image has a different initial sound, and the child must find the odd one out and say why it is the odd one out.

Wolfy, Wolfy, What's the Sound?

This game is great for playing outside. Tell the children Wolfy's secret sound. The children all line up behind you and walk around the playground chanting "Wolfy, Wolfy what's the sound?" When the wolf says the magic sound, the children all run away, and you try to catch the next wolf.

I Spy

Play I Spy using letter sounds. I Spy has several variations; it can be played with an I Spy Board, book, or the children guess objects in their immediate surroundings. You can also place small world objects into a bottle with rice, and the children guess from the objects in the jar.

Buried Treasure

Bury items that begin with the same initial sound in a sand tray. The children then dig up the things and say what they have found and the initial sound. You can also do this activity with two sets of items beginning with two different initial sounds. The children then dig out the things from the sand and say what the items are, the initial sound and then sort them into two sound groups.

Silly Soup

This game is a variation of the game found in the *Letters and Sounds* book, and children love it. Place objects or pictures of things with the initial sounds the children have learnt in a bowl. The children sit in a circle and pass the bowl around while singing the rhyme. When the rhyme stops, the child holding the bowl picks an object/picture out of the bowl, says the word and the initial sound.

I want to make some silly soup
I'm making soup that's silly
I want to make some silly soup
I'm making soup that's silly

Initial Sound Sort

Make a set of picture cards and a worksheet with a picture of an object with the initial sound you are teaching or revising. For example, you could create a worksheet with a sun on it and the children then find all the pictures of items beginning with an **s** from the stack of picture cards.

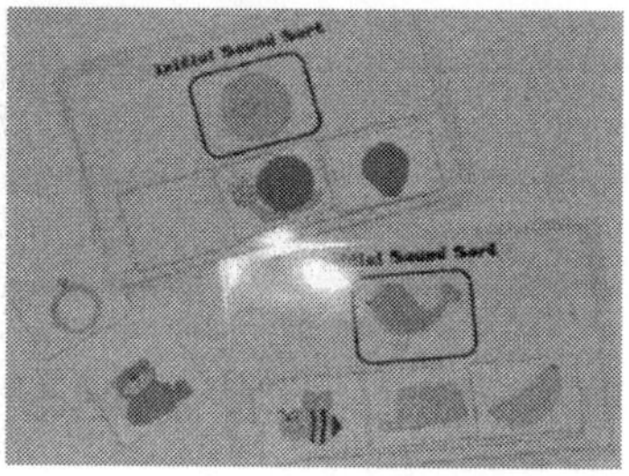

Tongue Twisters

Children love tongue twisters. There are plenty available online and even a few tongue twister books in print. Tongue twisters reinforce initial sound recognition and have the added benefit of doubling up as speech therapy for children who struggle to say certain sounds.

She sells seashells on the seashore.
Betty Botter bought some butter.
How much wood would a woodchuck chuck if a woodchuck could chuck wood?
I scream, you scream, we all scream for ice cream.

Do They Sound the Same?

Say a pair of words, and the children show you a thumbs up if the words begin with the same initial sound or a thumbs down if they do not.

Teacher: **bat/coat**
Children: (thumbs down)
Teacher: **bat/boat**
Children: (thumbs up)

Segmenting and Blending Phonemes

Children need to learn how to break words into their component sounds and then put them back together. These strategies will enable them to read unfamiliar words and spell difficult words on their own. Spend lots of time orally segmenting and blending words to build a firm foundation.

Robot Sounds

Call out a word and have the children say the sounds. The children pretend to be robots while they are sounding out the words and move their arms in short jerking movements bending at the elbow with each sound, we call these robot arms. For example, you say the word cat and the children say: "**c-a-t** (while using robot arms for each sound), **cat.**"

Silly Simon Says…

Play Silly Simon with the children but sound out the last word. The children then blend the sounds, say the word, and do the action.

Teacher: Silly Simon says stand **u-p.**

Children: **Up** (while standing up).

Teacher: Silly Simon says stamp your **f-ee-t.**

Children: **Feet** (while stamping their feet).

Cross the Road

Give each child a familiar object. Draw a road on the playground or in the classroom using chalk, then sound out a word, and the child with the object can cross the road.

"The **L-e-g-o** can cross the road (using the sounds, not letter names.)"

"The **c-ar** can cross the road."

Blending Cards

Print out a set of consonant letter cards on one colour card and vowel letter cards on another colour. Lay all the cards on the table upside down. The child then picks up two cards, one in each colour, places them together, says the sounds then blends the two sounds. Play this game daily until the child is confident and blends easily. You can then add some new sounds or get the child to pick up two consonant cards and place them on either side of the vowel and ask the child to blend the CVC word. If they still cannot do this then, go back to blending VC pseudo words until they are ready and then try again.

Count the Sounds

Say a word, then the children repeat the word, the second time they say the word they stretch out the word while counting the sounds on their fingers, then they say the word one last time.

Teacher: **Ship**

Children: **Ship**, **sh-i-p**, -three sounds (while holding up three fingers), **ship**.

Phoneme Buttons

Create phoneme button picture cards. Each card has the same number of buttons as the sounds in the picture, this helps the child to self-correct should they have the incorrect number of sounds. There is no writing or letters, just the awareness of sounds. The child sounds out the word by pressing each

button as she/he says the sound. If the child gets the snail picture card they say "**snail**," then they use their finger to touch each button as they say the sound in the word slowly "**s-n-ai-l**." To vary this activity the child could make four playdoh balls and place one on each phoneme button and then press into each ball as they sound out the words, some children may even enjoy smashing each ball with a fist as they sound out.

Phoneme Button Strips

Create phoneme button strips; these are the same as phoneme button cards except they are on strips of card. Remember children need to do the same activity several times for them to learn effectively, however if you present the activity in the same way each time, they will quickly get bored so varying the layout is one way we can recycle the activity. Each card has the same number of buttons as the sounds in the word to help the child recognise the number of sounds. The child presses each button on the strip as they sound out the word. If the child gets the moon strip they say "**moon**," then they use their finger to touch each button as they say the sound in the word slowly "**m-oo-n**." To vary this activity the child can place a cube or counter on each sound button and move the counter as they say each sound.

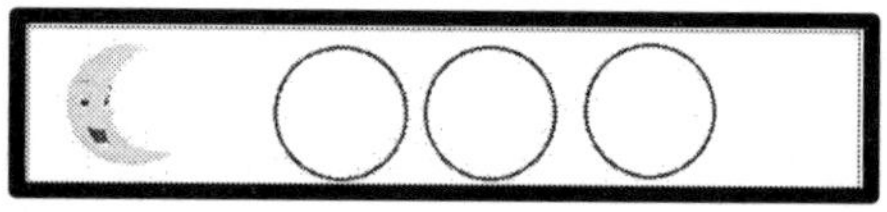

Puppet Language

Puppets are a great way of getting children's attention, if you find their attention has been waning or they are a little bored of phonics lessons then break out a Phonics Puppet. Tell the children an elaborate back story for your puppet and give him or her an interesting name like Philomena Phonics or Fabulous Fred Phonics. Then tell them that the Phonics Puppet sometimes gets confused and uses sounds instead of words, so they need to put the sounds back together to help you understand him. Then have the puppet sound out some words, and the children can say the words that the puppet is sounding out.
Puppet(teacher): I want some **l-u-n-ch**.
Children: **lunch**!

Move It

Give the children some manipulatives such as counters, cubes, or balls. Then say a word, the children repeat the word then slowly sound it out while moving one counter for each sound. They then count the counters and say how many sounds are in the word.
Teacher: **Bed**
Child: **Bed, b-e-d** (while moving counters), -three sounds.
To develop phonological awareness, you can then ask questions or give instructions about the word.
Teacher: Point to the middle sound.
Squash to the last sound
Move to the first sound back and say the word without it."

I Spy

Play I Spy with the children but sound out the word. You can play I Spy with objects, pictures, I Spy books, or I Spy bottles.
Teacher: I spy with my little eye a **d-o-ll**.
Children: **Doll**!

Picture Cards

Place cards with pictures of objects containing the sounds the children have learnt on the table face-up. The child picks up a picture card, says the word for the image, then says the sounds in the word. At first, the child may only say the first or last sound, if this happens repeat the word and sound it out with all the sounds so that they child can hear them, with time and repetition they will begin to hear the middle sounds as well
Child: "Fish, f-sh, fish"
Teacher: That's right, fish, f-i-sh, fish"

Sound Isolation

Say a word and have the children repeat the word, sound it out and say the word again. Then ask questions about the position of the sounds within the word.
Teacher: **Pig**
Children: **Pig, p-i-g, pig**.
Teacher: What is the first sound?
Children: **p**
Teacher: What is the last sound?
Children: **g**
Teacher: What is the middle sound?
Children: **i**

Sound War Cries

Use old-school style "war cries" to play call and repeat games. These are fun games to play outside as they can get a little rowdy. Remember to use the letter sounds and not the letter names.
Teacher: Give me an **f**!
Children: **f, f** you've got your **f**!

You can also develop their auditory memory and blending skills.
Teacher: Give me an **f**!
Children: **f, f**, you've got your **f**!
Teacher: Give me an **i**!
Children: **i, i**, you've got your **i**!
Teacher: Give me a **sh**!
Children: **sh, sh**, you've got your **sh**!
Teacher: What does that give you?
Children: **Fish, fish**, it gives you **fish**!

Consonant Blend Sound Counting

Say a blend such as **cl**. The children say the blend then segment it while counting the sounds on their fingers and lastly, they repeat the blend.
Teacher: **cl**
Children: **cl, c-l** (while holding up two fingers), **cl**.

They can also tell you a word containing the consonant blend. Use both initial and final blends.

Tactile Phonics Bean Bags

The children explore embroidered bean bags in open-ended play to reinforce the sounds learnt. They can sort the bean bags by sounds or say the picture on the bean bag and sound out the word.

The Alphabet

Teach children to say the alphabet rather than sing the Alphabet Song. When they sing the song **L, M, N, O, P** becomes one word and there is little separation between the letter names. This activity does not help them with their early phonics sounds it does help develop their auditory memory.

Phonics Tubs

Phonics tubs contain small world items that have the phoneme somewhere in the word. You can make your own tubs or by ready-made phoneme tubs. The phoneme is printed on the lid of the tub, and inside are the small world toys. These tubs are great for developing children's phonological awareness. They can also be used to introduce alternative graphemes. Give the children items from two or more tubs to sort into the correct tubs. Have them sound out the items, ask them questions about the position of sounds in the words, have them sort the items by initial, middle, and ending sounds or let them explore and play with the objects.

15 ACTIVITIES TO TEACH READING

Reading is the blending together of sounds represented by letters to form a word. Children need to move while learning to read, and it should be taught in a multi-sensory way. They need to engage with what they are doing, have fun and move to embed the new knowledge and skills.

Flashcards

Go through the flashcards with the everyday. These can be on a PowerPoint; they can be handheld cards or using interactive software like Phonics Play. Vary the presentation of these flashcards to keep the children interested.

Children need to be encouraged to read the flashcards as quickly and accurately as possible as rapid recall aids blending. Sometimes children get into the habit of dragging out the sound and say "**ayyyyyyyy**" instead of **ay** if this happens stop the flashcards and show the children how to make a crisp pure sound. If they drag out the sound, they will find it harder to hear the word when blending.

Sound Display

As a new sound is taught, it is added to the sound display in the classroom. Jolly Phonics has a freeze that can be bought and added to as the children learn new sounds, Twinkl has lots of phonics display ideas and THRASS has phonics display boards with all the consonant and vowel sounds. My favourite display option is the THRASS display as it is consistent and can be used throughout the school and the children's phonics charts are identical to the display chart.

Whichever display option you choose should be referred to throughout the day. Point to the sounds, and the children say the sounds or show the children on the alternate phonemes and graphemes to help them read unfamiliar words.

Reading Manipulatives

Children who are learning new information need to be physically active. Use small objects such as playdoh balls, cubes, or counters to represent phoneme buttons. The child uses one thing per sound and moves (or squashes if it is playdoh) the thing as they say the sound. For example, if the child sees the word rabbit, they should put one manipulative under each sound, they then read each sound and blend them together to say the word.

Dots and Dashes

Once children understand the concept of finding the sounds in words using physical manipulatives, they can then move on to drawing dots and dashes under the sounds in words. The child draws a dot under a graph and a dash under a digraph, trigraph or quadgraph.

Reading Material

Reading is important in all aspects of life and therefore it should not only be presented in books. Reading activities can be presented to children as letters, recipes, blogs, menus, notes, lists or road signs. Children need to read daily to make good progress so have a good reading incentive scheme to encourage reading at home and make use of volunteers to listen to readers in school.

Phonics Reading Books

Decodable books or phonics books are books that the child can read independently once they have learnt the appropriate phonemes and graphemes. These books give the child practice and consolidate new knowledge.

They are normally arranged into levels and are often assigned colours to demarcate these levels. The child moves up the colour bands based on their individual reading ability. Match the book to the child's book to their reading ability. An easy book will not challenge them while a difficult book will demotivate them. If a child can read roughly 80% of a book and decodes and blends the other 20% then you might want to try them on the next level of reading books. Use phonics books for whole class reading (to practice a new sound), small group reading in ability groups or one-to-one lessons with an adult.

Printable Phonics Books

There are lots of printable phonics books available online and children like making and reading their own books. These can be used to consolidate a new sound, encourage reluctant readers or as an alternative to published reading material to keep the reading lessons interesting.

Reading Booklets

Reading Booklets are small, short phonics books. They can be re-used, given to a child as a reward or personalised by inserting the child's name.

Picture Books

Reading starts with looking at books, then recognising letters and words and then reading sentences. Provide picture books in the reading corner as well as in a box for outside play. Children explore these books and slowly begin to discover that they can read them, and this improves their self-confidence and reading motivation.

Chapter Books

Place chapter books in the reading corner from Year One onwards. Good readers will discover they can read them, and this will boost their confidence. Good readers with visual tracking difficulties will struggle to read chapter books, have these children place a bookmark under each line as they are reading.

Letters

There are lots of opportunities for the children to read letters throughout the year. The children could get a letter from Father Christmas, the Easter Bunny, or the Elf on the Shelf. They could even get a personalised letter from the Tooth Fairy when they lose a tooth.

Labels

Label everything in the classroom including the furniture. Add signs, explanations, and questions to displays. Put spelling words up on display and use words as part of role play areas, like menus for a restaurant or price lists in a shop. Labelling the classroom provides opportunities for incidental reading.

Recipes

To vary reading lessons have the children read a recipe to bake or cook something. These types of activities are fun, and inspirational, they motivate children to read recipes on their own. Recipe books can also be part of the book corner and role play area.

Lists

Provide lists for the children to read, lists of activities for Golden Time, possible outdoor toys, or toys for free play. Try to make the lists pertinent to the child's life and experiences.

Invitations

Birthday or wedding invitations are always exciting. If a teacher is getting married have her bring in a copy of the invitation for the children to look at and read. Look at the elements of an invitation and discuss the expectations that are set such as the formality of the event, time, and importance of replying to the invitation.

Cards

Provide opportunities for children to read Christmas, Easter, birthday, and thank you cards. Encourage card giving and making in class as part of your classroom traditions and celebrations. Look at the format and elements of different genres of cards and think about the receiver and giver of the card.

Menu

Collect some takeaway menus from local restaurants for children to read during role play. You can also set up a reading lesson where the children pretend to be waiters or patrons at a restaurant, and they order food and discuss what they have ordered.

You can also put up the school lunch menu for the children to read. We all like to know what we are having for lunch, so this reading activity provides intrinsic motivation to read.

Road Signs

Go on a walk to look at road and shop signs in the local area or print out some signs. These should be words and symbols, as symbol recognition is an essential part of learning to read. Most children can read the symbol for MacDonald's years before they start formal reading lessons at school!

Food Boxes or Cans

Bring in interesting food boxes or packets to use as part of reading lessons. There are many lovely "stories" at the back of products used as part of the marketing for products. The cat food that I buy has a fabulous letter on the back from a cat called Phoebe who tests the cat food before it gets sent to market, it is a real-world example of writing for an audience, persuasive language, technical jargon, and the structure of a letter. Children love things like this, and it makes them explore (and read) other packets and boxes in the pantry at home.

Comics

Comics, or graphic novels, stimulate children's interest with their bright illustrations and action-packed storylines. Place comics in the book corner or use them as part of your reading lessons. They are also an excellent example of direct speech and use many different types of sentences. Comics can motivate reluctant readers and boys particularly enjoy superhero comics about their favourite characters.

Tablets or Computers

E-books or living texts are hugely popular with modern children who prefer them to dead texts (traditional paper books) as they are interactive. These books can be follow-along books (a narrator reads and the text lights up as it is read), read alone books (the child reads the book without help) or narrated/audible books (audio books without accompanying text). All these types of books have their uses, the trick is variety as the child can then develop the greatest range of skills.

Instruction Cards

Create instruction cards for the children to follow to complete tasks. You can also use ready-made instruction booklets like those that accompany Lego models. Remember that even though these booklets have few words, children must interpret the instructions from the beginning to the end, follow along step-by-step, concentrate, self-correction and problem solve. These are all essential reading skills. These also make great independent activities and are motivational for reluctant readers.

Word Cards

Create word cards for the children to read. These can be the Common Exception Words or based around a sound or phase. They can be used as flash cards, matched to pictures or the children can use them to practice segmenting and blending for the phonics screening.

Grapheme Recognition

Automatic grapheme recognition is essential for good reading and spelling. Children need to recognise the sounds for graphs, digraphs, trigraphs, quadgraphs and alternatives both in isolation and in words.

Letter Auction

Letter auctions are a great end of the week revision exercise. Each child gets a set of lolly sticks. On each stick is a circle with the each of the sounds learnt during the week printed on the circle so that the lolly sticks resemble auction paddles. Sit all the children down and then call out a sound, and the children raise the correct paddle and repeat the sound back to the teacher. The children love it if you use a silly auctioneer voice and style for this activity.

Teacher: I'm looking for a **b, b**, anyone have a **b**?

Children: **b!**

Alphabet Acorns

Alphabet Acorns are a commercially available game that reinforces letter recognition. Each plastic acorn is a tiny bottle and lid that contains a phonetic toy. Use the acorns for sorting, arranging to form words, matching the letter to the object, or teaching alphabetical order.

Phonics Pebbles

Collect some pebbles at the beach and write graphemes on the pebbles or buy Phonics Pebbles from consortium. The benefit of the commercially available pebbles is that the children can touch and feel the graphemes that are etched into these pebbles. The pebbles can be sorted into phoneme groups, used to make words or you can say a sound, and the child finds the correct pebble sound. Play a game with the pebbles, place all the stones upside down on the table; the child then picks a pebble, turns it over and says the sound.

Fastest Is the Winner

Sit in a group with the children and hold up a sound; the child that says the letter the fastest is the winner and keeps the card. Play this game in ability groups so that lower ability children do not become disheartened.

Surfing Sounds Beach Ball

Surf balls sounds are a fun way to get the whole classes attention at the beginning of the lesson. Write some graphemes on a beach ball then throw the ball to a child. The child looks at the ball, chooses a sound, reads it, and throws it back to you.

Pouncing Game

Play this game in a small group, lay the graphemes face-up on the table and then say a sound, the children then pounce on the letter by slapping down their hands as fast as they can. You can also print the graphemes out big and place them on the floor and the children then jump on the graphemes.

Roll and Read

This activity develops automatic recall. Create some roll and read boards with the graphemes learnt so far in rows and a picture of the numbers on a die at the beginning of each row. Each child throws the die and then reads the letters associated with the number on their game board. This game can be played in pairs, or small groups and they can all have the same game board or boards targeting their specific needs.

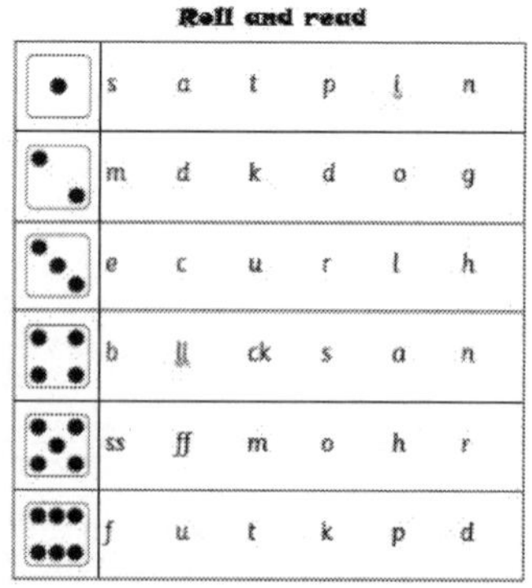

Letter Picture Bingo

Make or download some Bingo Boards consisting of the graphemes the children have learnt. Create a separate set of cards of pictures of objects beginning with the sounds the children have learnt. Every child in the group has a turn to be the caller, they pick an image from the picture cards, say the word and the initial sound, and anyone with that sound cover their letter with a counter on their board. The first child to cover their board is the winner. The picture cards can later be replaced with grapheme cards, the caller would then pick a card and say the grapheme and all the children with that grapheme cover the grapheme.

Sound Detectives

Give every child a magnifying glass then tell them they are going to be detectives and they must find some missing sounds in a book. Tell the children which sounds they are looking for or write down the graphemes for the children. To ensure the children experience success in this activity, give them books containing the target sounds; the *Bug Club Books* have a list of the phonemes at the back of each book which make them ideal for this activity. A variation of this game is to print a text, called a phoneme spotter, containing the sounds and then give each child a highlighter, and they highlight the words containing the target graphemes.

Swat It Game

Print a set of grapheme cards and lay them face-up on the table, then say a sound the children then swat the card with a fly swat.

Grapheme Memory Game

Print a set of cards with the graphemes learnt so far and another set of cards with pictures beginning with the sounds learnt. Place all the cards upside down on the table. The children take turns to turn over two cards; if they get a pair, they can keep it. If they do not get a pair, they turn them back over.

To vary this activity use pairs of matching letters, lowercase and capital letters, or pairs of pictures and word cards.

Picture Cards

Print cards with pictures containing the sounds the children have learnt and another set of cards with the graphemes learnt on the table. Each child picks up a picture card; says the word for the image and the initial sound and finds the matching grapheme card. If the child does this easily, have them pick up and read the grapheme card first and then find the corresponding picture card.

Turnover and Say

Print a set of grapheme cards and lay them upside down on the table. The children take turns to turn over the cards and say the sounds. If they say the sound correctly, they can keep the card; if not, they turn it back over.

Sound Snap

Create a set of grapheme cards, print each card twice to create a matching pair. Or create matching pairs by printing a picture and the grapheme for the initial sound in the picture. For children learning Phase Five Sounds create pairs using alternate graphemes for the same phoneme, for example ai and ay would make a matching phoneme pair. The children then share out the cards and play Snap using the cards.

Shuffle and Deal

Print a set of graphemes and share them out between the children. Each child lays their sounds out in front of them face up. They then take turns to say their sounds as fast as possible. You could also say a words and the children say if they have any of the sound in the word.

Teacher: Sheep
Child 1: I have a p.
Child 2: I have sh.
Child 3: I have ee.

Pick Up and Pass

Print a set of graphemes to create cards and place them face-up on the table. Call out a sound and have a child pick up the sound and pass it around. Each child says the sound as they pass it around the circle. The last child places the sound back on the table.

Stomp Game

Print out graphemes large on A4 or A3 paper and lay them face-up on the floor. Say a sound, and the children find the grapheme and then stomp on the sound. This game is great for some outdoor learning.

I Went to The Zoo, and I Saw

Give each child an alphabet strip to help them play this game. You can start the game by saying the rhyme: I went to the zoo, and I saw an, then fill in the name of an animal beginning with the letter **a** (use the sound and not the letter name). The next person says the rhyme, the animal that started with the letter **a** and thinks of their own animal beginning with the letter **b**.

Treasure Hunt

Print a set of graphemes and place them around the playground or classroom. The children then go on a treasure hunt to find them. When they find them, they say the sound; if they get it correct, they can have a point for finding the grapheme and a bonus point for saying the sound correctly.

Sound Dash

Print graphemes in a large font on A4 or A 3 paper and place them in conspicuous places around the playground. Call out a sound, and children then dash to the sound. For a bit of variation, call out a movement and a sound.

Teacher: Walk to the **b**.
Teacher: Hop to the **l.**
Teacher: Skip to the **s**.

Letter Wands

Create magic letter wands by gluing plastic letters onto a lollipop stick. The children then walk around the classroom or playground, trying to find things that contain that sound.

Long Vowel Sounds Puzzles

Smart Kids have alternate grapheme puzzles, for vowels the game is called Long Vowel Sounds and for consonants it is called Consonant Sounds. These puzzles join to form sound families and are an excellent way to revise and reinforce alternate graphemes.

Word Tasks

Word activities begin with VC and CV words, then CVC. Before moving on to CVCC and CCVC words, spend some time on initial and final consonant blends. If children struggle to blend, go back to oral blending, and then progress onto letter blending activities and then words.

Blends Match Bingo

Make or buy a Bingo Board with consonant blends. The caller picks a card, says the blend and the children with the blends cover their graphemes with a counter. Have an adult should supervise this game as blends are difficult for children to read, say and hear, and the children may need support.

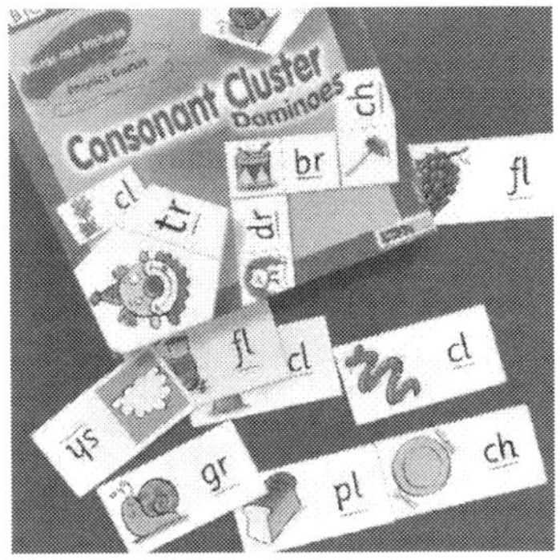

Blending Dominoes

Make or buy blending domino cards. On one side of the domino is a picture and on the other is a blend. The children then play dominoes by matching the blends to the pictures.

Talisman Card Games

Talisman Card Games are available from PhonicBooks. The cards come in sets that focus on a few sounds and are progressive. It is a simple card game that requires the players to read the words on the cards as part of the game. They have beautiful graphics, and older children will love them as the illustrations are modern and age appropriate.

Chunky Monkey Cards

Create a table with VC blends or write the blends onto a whiteboard. The child reads each blend from left to right. Repeat this activity regularly until the child reads the VC pseudo words quickly and easily. Once they have over-learnt VC chunks, you can then start on CV chunks. The idea is for the child to recognise chunks of words quickly and accurately and decrease segmenting and blending. Ensure the child is reading the letter sounds and not the letter names. You can then add consonants to the end of each set of letters to make CVC pseudowords or add new graphemes onto the table. This strategy is beneficial for children with Dyslexia.

sa	se	si	so	su
ta	te	ti	to	tu
pa	pe	pi	po	pu

Word Object Matching

Print a set of words that correspond to a group of objects. Each child picks a word, sounds it out, blends it and then selects the item off the table.

Word Picture Matching

Print a set of words that correspond to a group of pictures. Each child picks a word, sounds it out, blends it and then chooses the image off the table. Smart Kids has this game available as a puzzle. This activity can also be laid out as a worksheet with the child drawing a line to match the picture to the word.

Spelligator

Spelligator is a commercial game that is played in small groups and can be differentiated by phase. The game contains a word list so children can play independently and self-check their answers.

Reading Blocks

Write sets of words onto Lego or Duplo blocks. The children read the words written on the blocks and then sort them. The children can sort the blocks into rhyming words, initial sounds, final sounds, word families or vowel groups.

Picture Cards

Print a set of grapheme cards and a set of picture cards. Place all the cards on the table face-up. The child picks up a picture card, says the word and sounds it out, then finds the word card. If the child does this easily, they can pick up and read the word card first and then find the corresponding picture card. Alternatively, you can place the picture cards upside down, the child picks a picture card and then find the word card.

Buried Treasure

Print decodable words on coins and bury them in a sand tray. The children then dig for treasure and read the words before putting them into a treasure chest.

Minute to Win It

Place a set of decodable words on the table. The child sounds out and blends as many words as possible in a minute using a sand timer. They keep all the correctly read words, and the child with the most cards wins the game.

Reading Block Spinners

Reading block spinners are a Montessori reading aid, they come with sets of picture and word cards. The children spin the blocks to make words and then match the block spinner to the word card and picture card. You can than ask the child to say or write a sentence with the word.

CVC Toolbox

Children use tri-blocks (prism shaped interlinking cubes) to build CVC words to match picture cards. The cards are colour coded to help the children identify the letters needed to make the words.

Robot Arms

The children pretend to be robots and they move their arms in jerky movements from the elbow. They then segment the word and with each sound they move their arms like a robot, once the word is segmented, they then blend it to say the word.

Race Car Reading

Make a picture of a road and laminate it so that you can write on it with a whiteboard marker. Write decodable words onto the racetrack, making sure there is a small space between each grapheme. The child then drives their toy car slowly over the graphemes saying the sounds as they move from left to right in their "Practice Drive". They then get ready to race; when they race their car, they must drive over the sounds again but much quicker this time. The race officials are listening; they need to hear all the sounds and the word at the end, or the driver will be disqualified!

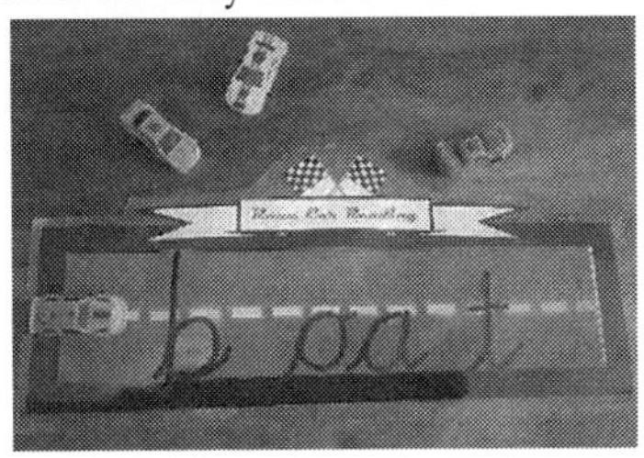

Child: **c-oa-t** (Slowly driving a car over the first time.)
Child: **c-oa-t, coat** (Quickly driving while sounding out the word again and then says the word.)

Word Cards

Print a set of decodable word cards and place them face up on the table. Each child picks a card, sounds it out and reads the word. Once the children can read the words confidently, they can play the game again with the words face-down so that they cannot see the word before they read it.

Phoneme Flip Stand

Phoneme flip stands by Smart Kids have CVC letter cards and picture cards on a spiral stand. The child makes the word for the corresponding picture, providing you with evidence that the child understands what they have read. They can also make real and nonsense words giving them valuable practice for the phonics screening.

Train Track Blending

Tell the children they are going to train to be train drivers. Write graphemes onto stickers and stick them onto a train track to form words leaving a space between each grapheme. The child drives their train slowly over the graphemes saying the sounds as they drive from left to right in their "Practice Drive." Then then drive their train over the graphemes again a little bit quicker until they can hear and say the word. Then they have passed their "Train Driver's Licence."

Fastest Is the Winner

Hold up a word, the child that says the word the fastest is the winner and keeps the card. Play this game in ability groups so that lower ability children do not become disheartened.

Word Books

Print or write a set of words with a common grapheme onto strips of paper. Make a cover for the book with the grapheme printed on the front and staple the words together. The child then reads through the words each day until they are confident with the grapheme, they can then move on to the next book. This activity is good for children with Dyslexia as there is only one grapheme to learn, on word on each page, lots of repetition and moving through the books gives them a sense of achievement. They can also think of sentences with the words, draw the words or write the words.

Picture Word Puzzles

Print a set of pictures with the name of the image printed underneath. Cut the pictures into puzzles by separating the graphemes. The children then build the puzzles to make the word. There are lots of commercially available words puzzles and some of these are self-correcting so children can work independently.

Catch A Word

Children love ball games, I always use a beach ball for phonics activities as no-one can get hurt and nothing can get broken, I learnt the hard way! Say a phonetically decodable word then throw the ball to a child, and they say the initial sound, they throw it to the next child who says the next sound, and the children keep throwing the ball to each other until the word has been sounded out. The last child says the word and throws the ball back to you.

Teacher: **brush**.
Child 1: **b**
Child 2: **r**
Child 3: **u**
Child 4: **sh, brush**

Trash or Treasure

Print a set of words; some of the words are real, and others are pseudowords. Place a bin and a crown on the table. The children read the words, if the word is a real, they put it by the crown; if it is a nonsense word, they put it in the bin.

Word Puzzles

Give the child a word; they then cut it into the sounds and remake the word. This activity is beneficial when children are learning new digraphs and trigraphs. Give the child the word **sheep**; they cut it into **sh-ee-p** and remake the word. Print the digraphs in a different colour to make it easier for the child to see, then later, the colour cues can be removed.

Read and Reveal

Give the child a word card on a strip of paper, the right-hand side of the paper is folded over to hide a picture. The child sounds out and reads the word, then looks at the picture to find out if they read the word correctly. This is a good self-correcting task that builds confidence in young readers.

Key Ring Book

Create key ring books of word families. The cards each contain an initial graph and a picture of the word, the word ending is on the last card. The child flips over each card to read another word, this activity reinforces rhyming words and is self-correcting because of the pictures.

Flip Flap Book

Make or download a flip-flap book. On the left of the flip-flap book is a set of initial graphemes stapled together. The child flips open the initial sound, reads the word, and finds the corresponding picture card that is stapled onto the right-hand side of the book. This is a good way to assess if the child understands what they are reading.

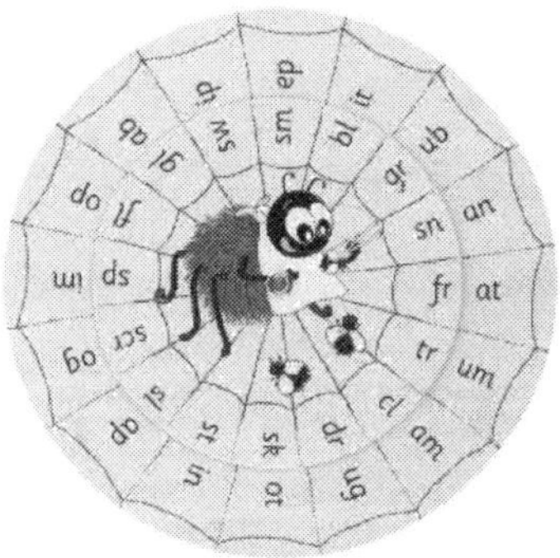

Word Wheel

Make word wheels from paper plates by writing initial graphemes on a small inner plate and word ending on a large outer plate. The child moves the centre plate to make and read words. They can then make the word with magnetic letters, write it, or say a sentence with the word. *Jolly Phonics* has word wheels with initial blends, and Twinkl has various types of word wheels.

Word Slider

Make or buy word sliders. The child moves a strip of card to change one letter to make new words. They can then make the word using magnetic letters, write it, or make a sentence with the word. *123 Homeschool4me* has some beautiful printable word sliders.

House Building

This game is suitable for sorting alternate sounds. Write words with alternate graphemes onto lolly sticks and place them on the table. Cut out two (or more if you are doing more graphemes) triangles and write the graphemes on the triangles, these will form the roofs of the houses. The child picks a stick, reads the word, and then places it under the correct roof.

Wordsearches

Create wordsearches with the grapheme the children are learning using puzzle maker software. Start with small word searches with a few words in lowercase. Teach the children how to look for the first letter of a word then look around the letter to see if it makes the word. Children with Dyslexia and visual perceptual difficulties will find wordsearches very difficult.

Caption and Sentence Reading

Children learn to read and write short captions before they can read and write simple sentences. Not all the words in sentences and captions are decodable therefore it is important to teach children to read a few Tricky Words as this will give them greater access to reading materials.

Caption Reading

Model reading a caption the first few times until the children start to understand the concept. Show them a short caption and a picture. Sound out the first word and then blend it to read the word. Then sound out and blend the second word, then read the first and second word. Lastly, sound out and blend the third word and then read all three words in order. If there are any Tricky Words, point them out and tell the children the word.

Teacher: **b-i-g, big**
r-e-d, red. big red
b-u-s, bus, big red bus

Caption Picture Matching

Give the children a set of captions and a set of corresponding pictures. The children then match the captions with the related images. Smart Kids have this activity available as a puzzle.

Shared Reading

Read with the child by reading the parts of the test the child cannot access and then stopping at the decodable words and encouraging the child to sound out and read the word. Alternatively, the child can read a page or sentence, and you read a page or sentence.

Sentence Substitutions

Sentence substitutions are sentences where the nouns can be swopped for other nouns. There is a base sentence and then a set of noun cards, the child reads the original sentence they then choose other nouns to place over those in the original sentence to create a new sentence. This allows weak readers to practice the same sentence repeatedly to develop fluency and confidence. You can create a set of sentence substitution cards using the words and sentences at the back of the book or alternatively, Smart Kids produce sets of Sentence Substitution in different phases.

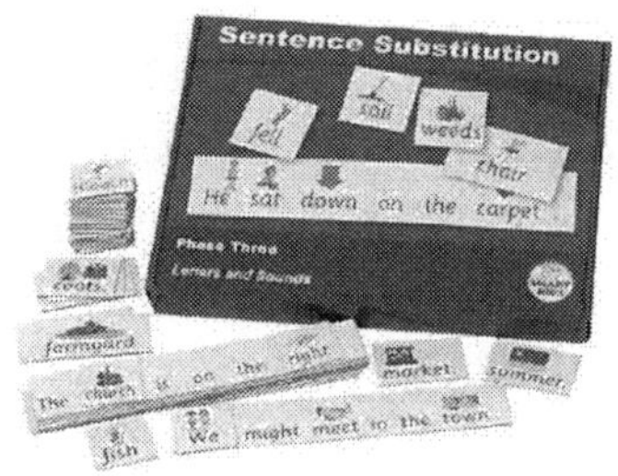

Sentence Toolbox

Children use word tri-blocks (interlocking prisms) with words printed on them to copy sentences from instruction cards. The sentence cards are colour coded to help struggling readers.

Picture Sentence Matching

Print out a set of pictures and matching sentences, the children match the sentences to the correct pictures. Smart Kids have this activity as a puzzle to add an element of self-correction, ensuring children experience success.

Sentence Scramblers

Sentence Scramblers is a Smart Kids resource where children use a colour spinner to pick colours and create sentences using the corresponding-coloured word cards.

Sentence Flip Stand

The sentence flip stand consists of words printed separately on cards and bound on a spiral stand. The children then flip the words over the stand to create sentences. The nouns have pictures, and the parts of speech are colour coded to help with comprehension. the understanding of sentence structure and the elements of a sentence.

Magnetic Words

Magnetic words are available everywhere from Amazon and E-bay to hobby and toy stores. The children use the magnetic words to build sentences. They often also come with blank pieces so that the children can write their own words. Write the child's name on one of the pieces so that they can incorporate their name into their sentences.

Reading Harder Words

Once children start reading, they encounter more complex words. These words may contain digraphs, trigraphs, quadgraphs, prefixes or suffixes; they could be polysyllabic or compound words, plurals, homophones, homonyms, or homographs. Children need strategies to read these new words.

Digraph and Trigraph Words

Show the children the new grapheme and model reading words containing digraphs and trigraphs. Give the children words containing the grapheme underlined or printed in colour as the children are still learning to identify digraphs and trigraphs in words. Then the children read the words containing the grapheme with adult support.

Boggled

a	r	i	l
p	d	f	o
o	t	s	n
k	e	w	m

Boggle

Boggle can be played using the actual Boggle Box, or you can make a Boggle board and print alphabet cards to use. The children write down as many words as they can. Words must be at least three letters long. The words can go in any direction, but all the letters must be connected in a chain, and each letter is only used once in a word. Plurals count as separate words.

So for this Boggled board they could find the words; wet, set, poke, pot, rap, if, rad, no, so, fir, par and rid.

Please do not play this game with children who have visual perceptual difficulties or Dyslexia, as they will find it very distressing.

Bananagrams

Buy or make a set of scrabble tiles or a Bananagrams game. Place all the tiles face-down on the table. Each child takes fifteen tiles. Everyone turns their tiles face-up and tries to arrange the tiles into intersecting word grids. Words must be read from top to bottom or left to right. They can rearrange their grid at any time and as often as they like. Whenever a player places their last letter face-up, that child calls out Peel! Then every player takes another tile. The first child to use all their letters in a connected word grid wins when there are no letters left in the pile. A child can play Bananagrams on their own. They place all the tiles face-down, take twenty-one tiles and play as usual.

Race the Clock

The teacher puts a list of words on the board. The children then read the words as fast as possible. Use the same words for a few days, and the children try to improve their time. This activity can be used for small group or individual work if the list is printed out for the child to read.

Stories to Teach Compound Words

Compound words are words made from joining two words together. The compound word butterfly is made from the words butter and fly. *Once there was a bull…(frog)* by Rick Walton and *Flying Butter* by

Patricia Trattles are fun-filled books that play with compound words. Children enjoy these books, and they lead to great discussions about words and vocabulary. Follow up activities to these books include finding all the compound words in the book, creating lists of compound words, or replacing the compound words in the story with other compound words.

Compound Word Addition

Compound words can be presented as addition equations. Children who enjoy math love this activity. Start by adding the two-component words to make the compound words. Once children understand the concept of compound words, you can give them the compound word, and they can find the two-component words.

butter + **fly** =___________

butterfly = ________+ ________

Compound Word Surgery

Tell the children there was a terrible accident in the morning involving a pair of scissors and some words, and the words were all chopped up. They need some brave nurses and doctors to put the words back together. Then give the children the compound words which have been cut into the component words and a box of plasters, and they put the words back together using the plasters. Feel free to give the children role play doctors and nurses outfits to enhance this activity- the more children enjoy an activity the more they will learn.

Magic e Wand

Write a list of CVC words that can be changed into split digraph words with the addition of an **e**. Make a magic **e** wand with a plastic **e** stuck on a lollipop stick. The child then uses the magic **e** wand and reads all the words as split digraph words by placing their magic **e** wand at the end of the word. The children can wear fairy wings or a wizards hat to make this activity more enjoyable.

CVC to Split Digraph Words

Create a list of CVC words that can be made into split digraph words with the addition of an **e**. Rewrite the words with space for an **e** on the end. The child then writes an **e** onto the end of the words to make them into split digraph words and rereads the words with the long vowel sound.

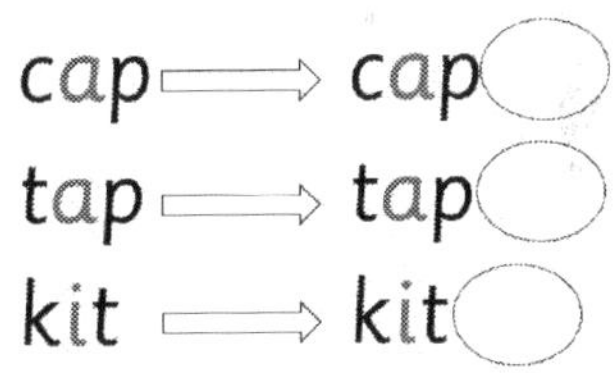

Split Digraph Folds

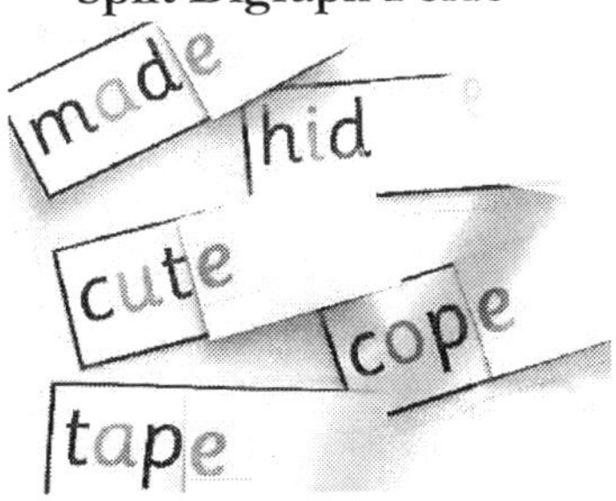

Write CVC words that can be made into split digraph words with the addition of an **e** onto strips of card. Make a fold on the end of the word and place an **e** on the outside of the fold. When the strip of card is folded over, it creates a split digraph word.

The child reads the word as a short vowel sound, then folds over the page and rereads the word as a split digraph word with a long vowel sound.

Split Digraph Ending In s

Children find it difficult to read split digraph plurals as the **e** is not on the end of the word. Write a list of words with split digraphs plurals, the children draw a box around the root word or draw a line to show the split digraph. They then read each word by segmenting the word correctly and reading the plural with a long vowel sound. I have seen a few split digraph plurals in the phonics screening over the years so this is an essential skill to learn in Year One.

mates	rates
makes	capes
tapes	cutes

Homographs Sentences

Homographs are words that are spelt the same but are pronounced differently. Teach the children about homographs and then give them sentences to read containing some common homographs. The child reads the sentence and decide how to pronounce the word based on contextual clues.

Wind up the hosepipe.
He will read to his teacher.
He shot the arrow with a bow.
She read the scary book in the dark.
The wind blew off his hat.
Bow when you meet the king.

He will read to his teacher.	
Wind up the hosepipe.	
He shot the arrow with a bow.	
Bow when you meet the king.	
She read the scary book in the dark.	
The wind blew off his hat.	

Homograph Pictures

Give the children a set of sentences containing homographs and the corresponding pictures. The children match the sentence with the correct image. Have each child read the sentences aloud to check pronunciation and comprehension.

Homographs Flip Book

The homograph flip stand consists of words and pictures printed on cards and bound on a spiral stand. This flipbook has a picture on the right and left of the word. The child then matches the two pictures to the word and then reads the word aloud twice while pointing at each picture as they read, this will check the child's understanding and pronunciation.

Homophone Flip Book

The homophone flip stand consists of words with a sentences printed on cards and bound on a spiral stand. Children find, all the homophones and then read, and compare the sentences.

Contraction Construction

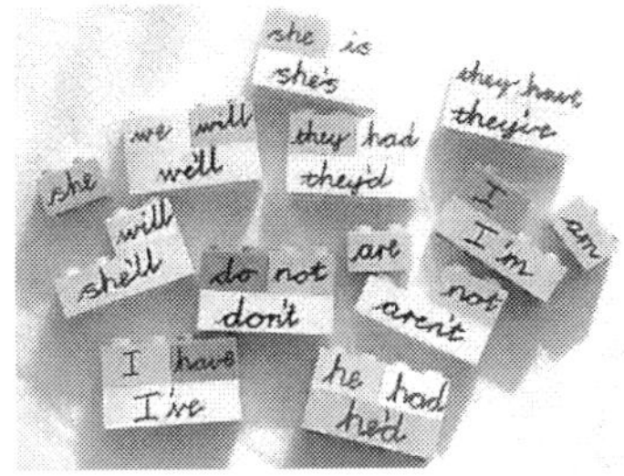

Write component words onto Lego pieces and the contraction onto a bigger piece of Lego. Give the Lego pieces to the children and have them build the puzzles.

Paint Strip Contractions

Write the two component words onto a paint strip and then fold the paint strip to make the contraction by writing the contracted form onto the end of the strip. The children read the two words then fold the strip of paper to read the contracted form.

Contraction Snowmen

Write the two words that are going to be contracted onto pictures of mittens. Then write the contracted form onto a snowman. The children then match the mittens to the snowman, they read the words separately and then read the contracted form.

Folded Contractions

The child folds a landscape piece of paper half and then in half again to create four columns. They then fold the two outside columns inwards so that they meet in the centre and look like wardrobe doors that can open and close. The child then writes the contracted form of the word on the inside of the wardrobe and the two component words on the outside of the wardrobe doors. If the paper is lined, you can write a list of contractions in this way.

Contraction table

Once children are familiar with contractions, they can complete a contraction table like the one in the word list at the back of the book. Put words that are commonly contracted at the top of each column and children can then sort and stick or write contractions into the correct columns. This activity categorises words and helps children make links between them and therefore learn to spell and read them easier.

will	are	is	not	have	had

Interactive Board Games

Interactive board games are an invaluable modern teaching tool. There are many great games available online; some are free, and others are paid, or subscription based. Phonics Play has both free and paid games. *Jolly Phonics* has interactive software that can be loaded onto the computer and *Twinkl* also has some phonics games.

Reading Strategies

These reading animals are wonderful way to teach children reading strategies for unfamiliar words. unfortunately, I cannot find the original author to credit for this great idea, but the children love it! One little boy said, "I really need this!" The animals have been adapted to fit with a phonetic approach to reading.

Reading Bookmarks

Make reading strategy bookmarks using the reading animals, the children can take these home and use them during reading lessons. Teach the children how to use the strategies, then focus on one or two strategies in a reading lesson or praise the child when they use one of the strategies. I find these bookmarks also help adults support children's reading.

Stretchy Snake: The child sounds out the word slowly, blends the sounds and says the word.

Chunky Monkey: They breaks the word into smaller parts or words then reads the word blending the parts.

Tryin Lion: They try reading the word another way using alternate phonemes.

Eagle Eye: The child looks at the pictures for clues.

Bouncing Bunny: They read the sentence skipping out the word, then come back and read the sentence filling in the missing word based on contextual clues.

Pointy Porcupine: They point to the words or sounds as they read.

Wise Owl: The child listens to hear if the word or sentence makes sense.

Reading Fluency

Reading fluency is what the child's reading sounds like when they are reading aloud. Reading should sound natural, like speaking. Fluent readers read accurately, use expression, pay attention to punctuation, have a natural pace, and vary their speed according to the mood or action of the text. They read in phrases, show intonation by raising or lowering their voices and use stress when reading words in italics or when emphasising a word in a sentence.

Reading for Fluency

Struggling readers and readers with Dyslexia will find sentence fluency particularly challenging. Create or download some fluency cards for the child to read. Each card consists of one sentence, the sentence is slowly built up, on the first line is the first word, the second line is the first and second word, on the third line is the first, second and third word etc. until the sentence is complete. This method gives students the repetition needed to develop fluency.

Hug
Hug the
Hug the rabbit
Hug the rabbit and
Hug the rabbit and the
Hug the rabbit and the cat.

Reading for Fluency with a Book

Explain to the child that you are going to practice fluency. Then demonstrate what fluency is by reading a sentence in a choppy robotic manner and then again in a fluent manner. Then pick an appropriate sentence in a book for the child to read. The text should not be too easy or hard for the child. Cover the sentence except for the first word with either a finger or a bookmark. The child reads the first word; the bookmark is then moved so that the second word is visible. The child starts the sentence from the beginning and reads the first and second word. The bookmark is then moved to reveal the third word, and the child reads the sentence from the start reading the first, second and third word in order, continue until the sentence is finished.

Whole-Class Reading

The whole class reads the same book, it is a slightly more advanced text than the year group reads typically. Every day the class spends some time reading together. Each child has a ruler, and they follow along in their books while the teacher reads, modelling good reading. Place weaker readers next to strong readers so that they can help them keep their place. This exercise exposes children to good quality text and teaches them reading expression, pace, fluency, phraseology, and intonation through modelling.

Individual reading

Find time regularly to read with each child individually. Assess their reading and adjust their reading level if necessary. Give the child specific teaching tailored to their reading needs during these times. Record what the child is doing well and date it so that there is evidence available should your year group be moderated.

Guided Reading

Guided reading is when the teacher teaches reading in a small group. The children are grouped according to their ability. One group reads with the teacher while the other groups do reading activities that they can complete quietly on their own or with a teaching assistant. Ensure the classroom is quiet and calm so that everyone can hear clearly.

For the teacher-led group, the children all get the same book or text. It is important that you read the text beforehand and finds any challenging sounds or words. Teach these words or sounds to the children at the start of the session. The children all get a turn to read while the others follow in their books by pointing at the words. You should also read as this provides the children with an opportunity to hear good modelling. The lesson should have a reading focus; this could be reading strategies, fluency, or comprehension. Decide on any questions before the lesson. Remember to formatively assesses during and after the lesson and record and date your observations of each child.

Reading Volunteers

Reading volunteers are a valuable resource; they sit and read with children individually, giving the child time to enjoy and explore the reading process. Reading volunteers can read with struggling readers or groups of children. Some schools ask reading volunteers to record what the child is doing well and date it for evidence, and others prefer this to be done by a teacher or teaching assistant. Keep a register of who has read with the volunteers.

DEAR

DEAR (Drop Everything and Read) is a great reading activity that the whole school can adopt. This activity is designed to foster a love of reading in children. Teach the children how to sit quietly, focus and read their books. When you first start DEAR times, you will need to lay out your expectations clearly, this is not a time to page through or look at books, the children are expected to be reading their books and therefore there should be no walking around or talking. The amount of time spent reading depends on the age group and the class, but a good guideline is about ten minutes. The teacher should also read during this time to model adults reading for enjoyment.

Punctuation

Teach children how to read punctuation. They should stop at a period, pause at a comma, show emotion at an exclamation mark and there should be a vocal inflexion at the end of a question. Model reading punctuation and have children practice these skills during guided reading.

Reading Comprehension

Reading comprehension needs to be taught. Children with good comprehension skills talk about what they have read; they summarise, compare the text to other books or their own experiences, make predictions or inferences and express an opinion on the text. Comprehension activities can be very dry and boring so try to think of exciting and engaging activities for the children to demonstrate and practise their comprehension skills.

Comprehension Bookmark

Give the children a bookmark with some comprehension strategies. During reading lessons focus on one or two strategies or ask the children to pick a strategy to discuss to show they have understood the text. The bookmark also supports teaching assistants and parents with comprehension questions when they are reading with a child.

Retelling Rat: The child retells what they have read in chronological order.

Connecting Crocodile: They talk about how the text relates to another text, the world around them or their own experiences.

Predicting Penguin: The child makes predictions about what might happen next in the text based on what they have read.

Questioning Squirrel: They ask questions about what they have read.

Inferring Insect: The child makes deductions about what they have read.

Visualise Vulture: The child visualises what they have read in their head.

Summarising Snail: They summarise the main ideas in their own words.

Journal

The child keeps a journal where they record their thoughts and opinions about the books they have read. Ideas for journaling include, drawing a picture of the text, writing a list of the, deciding what happens next, categorising things, summarising the story, retelling the story, or writing a book review.

Discuss

Facilitate a discussion with the children about the book. Ensure the children understand that their opinions about the text are neither right nor wrong if they can substantiate their statements with from evidence in the text. Even very young children can do this.

Categories

The child categorises information from the text by putting it into a table, a Venn diagram, or data sets; this can be on paper or with pictures or physical objects. For example, if the child has read a book about animals, they can use small world animals to put them into groups of happy and sad animals, or big and small animals, whatever categories fit with the text.

Draw

The child draws a picture about the text and then talks about the picture. Write a post-it note recording what the child has said, date and file it as evidence.

Drama

Give the children props and masks and let them act out the story. Write post-its and take photographs as evidence. The children demonstrate their comprehension though retelling, summarising, and expressing opinions of the text in an informal way.

Interview

Pretend to be a character from the story while the children interview you to find out more about the character's motives and actions. If this is done halfway through the text, the children could make predictions about what happens next based on the interview and what they know from the story.

Retell

Children read the story several times and learn to retell the story. They use actions and can either perform the story in the style of Pie Corbett's *Talk for Writing* or retell the story in small groups. Retelling a story helps children understand the text better.

Questioning

Encourage the children to ask questions about what they are reading. Teach them question words, then ask them, "I wonder what question we could ask about the story beginning with who /what/ where/ when/ how/ why?

16 EARLY WRITING

Writing is taught in stages; the first stage is mark-making, then patterns and picture drawing, letter writing, word writing, caption writing, sentence writing and then longer pieces. Most of the ideas used to teach writing and spelling can also be used to teach Tricky, Common Exception and High-Frequency Words.

Writing Implements

Expose children to a variety of writing implements and surfaces to encourage writing and exciting. Remember children learn the most when they are playing and having fun.

Pencil

Pencils come in different shapes and sizes. Fat, triangular pencils with grooves for fingers are better for younger children or children who struggle with fine motor control and are sold separately for right and left-handed learners. Pencils should always be sharp; they should only be sharpened on one end, and they should never be shorter than 10cm in length.

Pen

Pens come in different shapes, sizes, and ink types. Children love writing with pens; and they should be available for free play or special occasions.

Colouring Pencils

Colouring pencils come in a variety of sizes and shapes. Fat, triangular pencils with grooves for fingers are better for younger children or children who struggle with fine motor control and are sold separately for right and left-handed learners. Pencils should always be sharp; they should only be sharpened on one end, and they should never be shorter than 10cm in length.

Crayons

Crayons can be wax, plastic, retractable, pastel and come in various sizes. Crayons provide great sensory feedback. Short, stubby crayons are suitable for *Write Dance* activities and children with poor fine motor control.

Charcoal

Charcoal can be made or bought. It provides lots of sensory feedback especially if children write on sugar paper and is a great way to encourage children to explore mark making.

Highlighters

Highlighters come in a variety of colours, shapes, and sizes. Let children have access to highlighters during free play or when looking for graphemes on Phoneme Spotter Texts.

Felt tips

I am not a huge fan of felt tips, but children love them. They should not be used in books as they bleed through the paper. Provide felt tips for special occasions or activities or during free play.

Glitter

Children love glitter and you can now buy environmentally friendly glitter. They can write using a glue stick and then sprinkle glitter on top or write with a glitter glue sticks or liquid glitter glue. Keep an adult nearby so that your classroom does not end up looking like a Christmas party!

Whiteboard Markers

Whiteboard markers come in a variety of colours, nib types and thicknesses. The medium black pen from consortium seems to last the longest and is the easiest for children to handle. Teach children how to replace the lid on whiteboard markers, or you will go through hundreds!

Washable Markers

Children can write on glass surfaces such as classroom windows or mirrors with washable markers. They can trace patterns, letters, or words by Blu-tacking the instruction card onto the glass.

Piping Bag

Fill a piping bag with coloured icing. The children then decorate biscuits, cakes or crackers and write on them using icing; this is an enjoyable activity for Baker Day or to make celebration biscuits for Mother's Day, Father's Day, or Christmas.

Paint and Paint Brushes

Provide the children with different types of paint, acrylic, poster, and watercolour. Add salt to the paint to make it shiny in the sun. Flour in the paint makes it thicker and adding PVA glue to paint makes it stick to unusual surfaces. Add washing up liquid to paint to make it easier to wash out of clothing. Water is also an excellent "paint," give children a bucket of water on a warm day and let them paint words or letters onto the playground.

Provide children with different sized and textured paintbrushes. Anything can be used as a paintbrush, earbuds, toothbrushes, rollers, sponges, or fingers. Toys also make great paintbrushes; dip toy cars in paint and paint with the wheels or use dolls' hair. Cut shapes out of potatoes using cookie cutters and use them as stamps.

Chalk

Chubby chalk is excellent for pavements, while thinner chalk works well on chalk boards. Chalk provides excellent sensory feedback; however, children who do not like messy hands will find it challenging and sometimes even upsetting.

Writing Surfaces

Use different writing surfaces to keep children motivated and engaged in writing. Children with particular needs may prefer certain surfaces; children with colour stress due to Dyslexia will prefer a non-white surface, while those on the autistic spectrum may select a specific surface due to the sensory feedback it provides.

Paper

Provide children with different types of paper to keep them interested. Give them different sized and textured paper. They can write on paper muffin cups, paper plates or paper bags. They can even make their own paper to write their name on as a special Mother's or Father's Day gift. Children can use tracing paper or Baking Paper to trace their names, letters or writing patterns.

Cardboard

Give children access to cardboard in different sizes, textures, and colours. Have cardboard available for free play or use it for special writing activities. Thin cardboard is suitable for cutting activities when children are first learning to cut as it is easiest for children to hold while cutting.

Rainbow Scratch Paper

Scratch paper is great for children who press too lightly when writing as they will have to press harder to scratch off the surface. It is a good way to encourage reluctant writers to mark make.

Whiteboards

Wooden whiteboards are heavy, but they last the longest, and they are the easiest to clean. Plastic whiteboards that are plain on one side and lined on the other are the most useful as children can write on the lines. Temporary whiteboards can be made by laminating plain paper.

Sensory Writing Tray

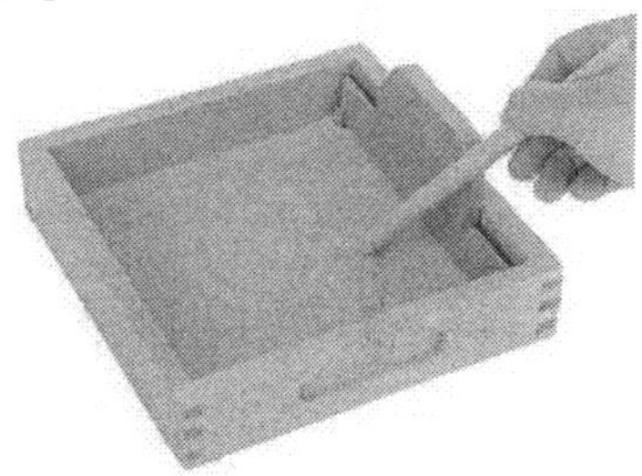

Line a shallow tray with sand or another sensory substance and have children write into the substance with a wooden pen or their fingers. Look for Montessori writing trays online as these are usually good quality, easy to store, and the children love them. Use hundreds and thousands, sand, flour, salt, rice, or sugar as sensory materials to line the tray.

Chalkboard

Chalkboards come in different shapes and sizes. Thin sheets of wood can be painted with chalkboard paint and mounted to the wall, wall writing builds shoulder stability and children love to use them to play teacher. Write graphemes on mini and place them next to each other to build words. Slate boards are made from rock and provide children with great sensory feedback.

Magnetic board

Magnetic boards are cheap and available at most toy stores or online. The children use a "pen" to write and then erase the board when they are finished. Have magnetic boards available for free play or use them for small group work or special writing activities.

Magnetic Writing Gel Boards

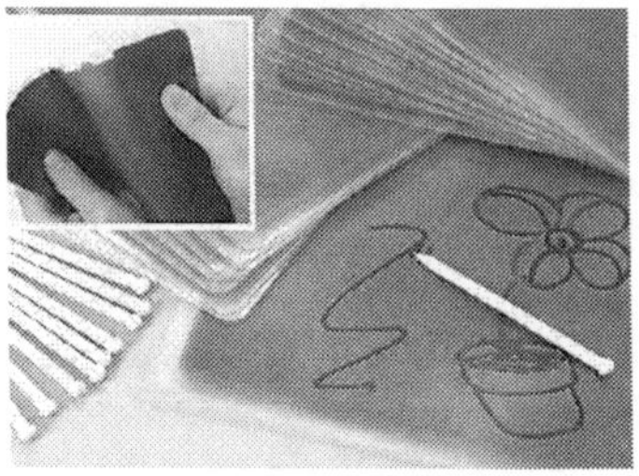

Magnetic Gel Writing Boards are available from Consortium. The children use the stylus provided to write on the boards. They then erase their writing with their finger.

Playdoh or dough

The child rolls out the dough to make a flat surface and then writes into the dough using a wooden skewer. Aid vanilla or peppermint essence to homemade dough to add another sensory component to the activity.

Post its

Most children cannot resist the urge to write on post-its; it makes them feel like the teacher. They can write lists, use them in free play or create notes for each other. Post-its come in different shapes, sizes, and colours, some are lined, and others have exciting watermarks.

Wooden Writing Boards

Wooden writing boards look like a slice of the trunk of a tree, they are sealed so that they can be used as whiteboards with dry-erase pens. The texture of the wood heightens the children's senses and enhances learning. These are wonderful for outdoor classrooms, Montessori, Waldorf or Reggio, and nature-inspired classrooms.

Tablets and Computers

Children love tablets. They can write or type their words on a tablet, i-pad, desktop or computer using a typing programme or write them on notepad or paint. Children with Dysgraphia will benefit from learning to use a keyboard.

Writing Tablet

Children write on LCD writing tablets just like traditional whiteboards and can rub out their writing when they are finished. They have bright, fun colours that the children enjoy and are reasonable robust.

Illuminated Writing Board

Illuminated light boards have different lighting settings and engage reluctant writers. Children on the Autistic Spectrum may particularly enjoy or dislike this writing surface.

Writing Bags

Put a small amount of paint or another substance in a bag and then seal the bag with duct tape so that it cannot leak. Children then write on the bag with their fingers or a earbud by displacing the substance inside. Suitable substances for writing bags are thickened paint, hundreds and thousands or rice. Make sure you place this activity outside or on a surface that is easy to clean if the bag breaks.

Squidgy Shapes

Squidgy Shapes are typically used for teaching shape, but they also make great writing surfaces. The children write onto the shapes with their fingers displacing the liquid and glitter inside.

Sensory Surfaces

Spread shaving soap, chocolate pudding or washing up liquid onto a flat surface, and the children write into the substance with a finger. Ensure this activity is closely monitored by an adult so that the children do not ingest anything they should not.

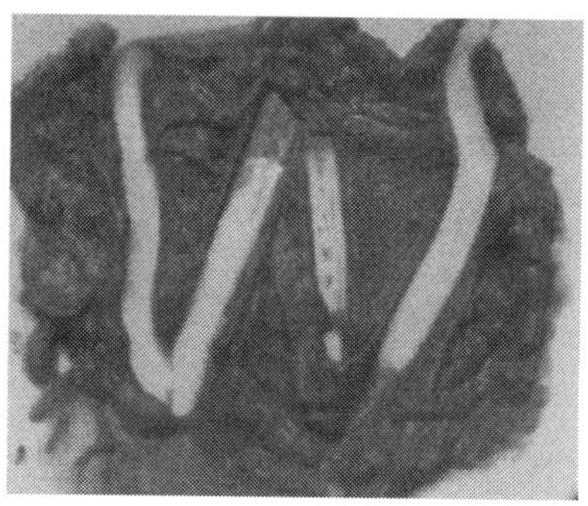

Letter Manipulatives

Learning is optimised when children move, physically engage with their learning, and use their senses. Give the children letter manipulatives to make their spelling words; this keeps learning fun, engages their thinking skills, and reduces worksheet overload. If you need evidence of their learning, take a photo of their task on top of their book (so that you know who's work it is) and stick it in their workbook.

Letter Cookie Cutters

Give the children different types of dough, bread dough, biscuit dough, playdoh, salt dough or homemade playdough. They can then roll the dough flat and cut out letters from the dough using alphabet cookie cutters. Alternatively, the children roll the dough into a sausage and use it to form letters.

Bread dough can be baked so that the children can eat their letters, this adds another layer of sensory input to the learning. Salt dough can be baked, painted, and sealed, and children can keep their letters and words. Add peppermint or vanilla essence to homemade playdough to enhance the sensory experience.

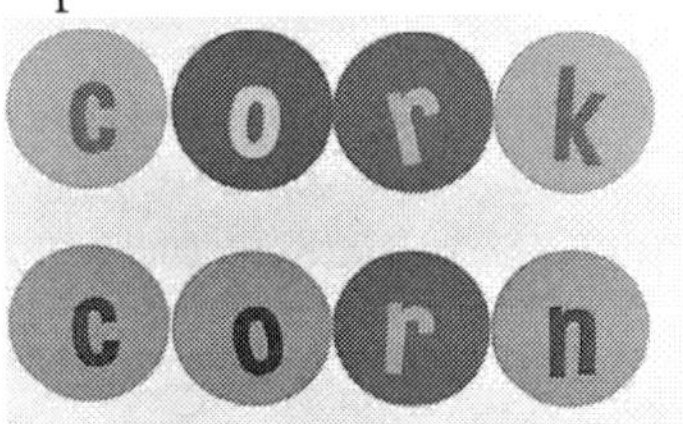

Alphabet Stickers

Children use alphabet stickers to make words. Stickers come in different shapes, sizes, colour, fonts, and cases. Children love this activity, and it can be used as an incentive or reward.

Alphabet Beads

Beads with letters printed on them are ideal for making words. Beads come in different colours, sizes, and cases. Children find it easier to thread beads onto pipe cleaners than string. They can copy word cards, make up their own words or create rhyming words. When children are first learning to spell their own names, they can make a bangle or necklace with their name on to keep.

Alphabet Stamps

Children use stamps to make words. Stamps come in different sizes and fonts. In addition, the children could also use different coloured stamp pads.

Wicki Sticks

Wicki sticks are thin strips of wax that children can manipulate to create 2D and 3D shapes. The children can bend the sticks to create letters and words. Remember to give the child the words or letters you want them to make as it takes a huge amount of processing for a young child to try to imagine the shape of the letter, create the letter and then form the word. Photograph the children's work to keep as evidence.

Felt Letters

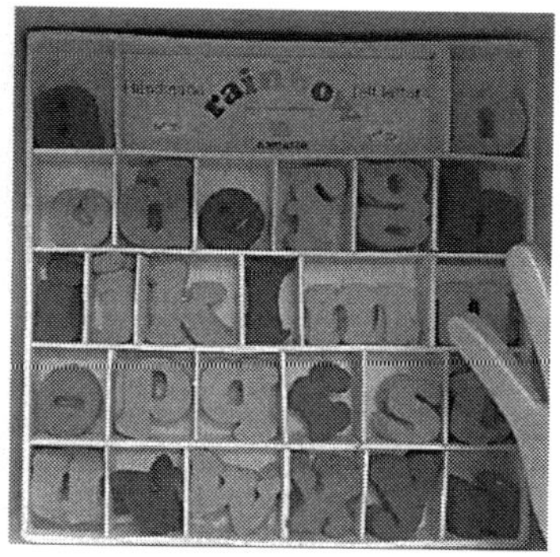

The children can use felt letters on a felt board or the carpet. You can say a sound, and the children find the correct grapheme. The children can put the letters into alphabetical order or separate the consonants from the vowels or they can arrange the letters to form words.

Alphabet Pasta

Alphabet pasta is a fun way for children to spell words. They can stick the words on paper with PVA glue, or you can photograph their learning for evidence. I suggest photographing the work and re-using the pasta as it is very hard to source and incredibly expensive, so I prefer to keep the pasta for a couple of lessons. Pasta comes in different cases so check that you have not bought capital letters, early writers as well as those with visual processing difficulties and Dyslexia will not be able to form words with capital letters as they have learnt to recognise lowercase letters.

Blocks

A variety of blocks can be used to form letters and words, Lego, Duplo, link bricks, unifix cubes, wooden bricks, or Meccano. The children form the letters using the blocks to create the shape of the letters.

Alternatively, write the letters onto the blocks and the children then lock the blocks together to form the words. Give the children a card with the word printed, as it is hard for children to think of words and then make them with blocks.

Keyboard

Use a real keyboard or one printed on a piece of paper. Give the children words cards with the words you would like them to practice, and they type the words onto the keyboard. Alternatively you can log on to a typing programme such as Word and let the children type their words and then print them.

Wooden Letters

Wooden letters are available from craft stores or Consortium. They are robust and will last for years. The children create words using the letters and then trace around them or write the words. Wooden letters come in different sizes, fonts, cases, and colours.

Peg Boards

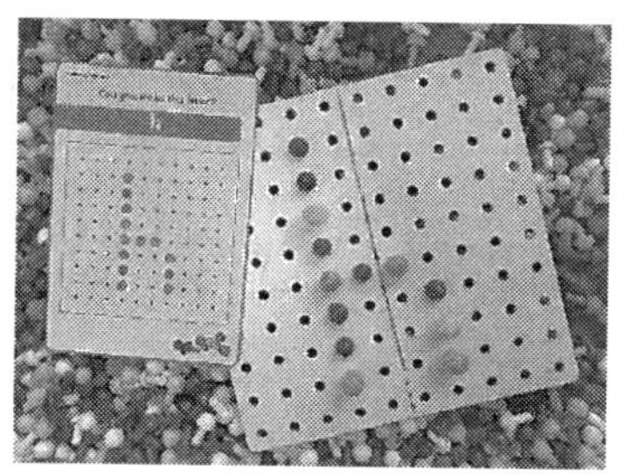

Children form letters or words using pegs. Give the child the word or letter to copy from or download pegboard letter instruction cards from *Twinkl.* Children with visual processing difficulties and Dyslexia will struggle with this activity.

Letter Tiles

The children can use letter tiles to create words. These can be coasters with letters printed on, Scrabble, Bananagrams or craft letter tiles. Carboard letter tiles can be printed from the computer. Before using letter tiles check if they are lowercase or uppercase as early writers, those with visual processing skills and children with Dyslexia will struggle to make words with capital letters if they have been taught to recognise lowercase letters.

Magnetic Letters

Children use magnetic letters to make words. Magnetic letters come in different colours, sizes, fonts, and materials. Coogam have a set of foam magnetic letters come in blue for vowels and red for consonants, each letter has the capital and lowercase form and they stored in a box with the letters alphabetised into compartments. I love these and is the one resource I would recommend over all others (I have two sets that I use every week). However, the children cannot trace around them because they stain, and they are not as robust as plastic magnetic letters.

Matchsticks

Children form letters and words using matchsticks, these can be bought at any craft store. Give the child an instruction card with the words or letters printed on so that they have a reference when doing the activity.

Newspaper Letters

Print a variety of letters from the computer or let the children cut letters from newspapers and magazines. They then form words using the letters. Make the activity more engaging by telling the children the words are a secret code or a ransom note, and they are spies creating a secret list of words.

Dotting Objects

The child uses gems, skittles, jelly tots, dot stickers, buttons, or bingo stamps to place over letters or words.

Letter Threading

Letter Threading is different to alphabet beads as they are the shapes of the letters. The children thread phonics beads onto a string to make words on the word cards. The word cards have pictures to help children understand the correspondence between words and meaning.

Pipe Cleaners

Children bend pipe cleaners to form letters and words. These letters can be kept in a tub and used again on another occasion. Remember to give the children the letters or words you would like them to make.

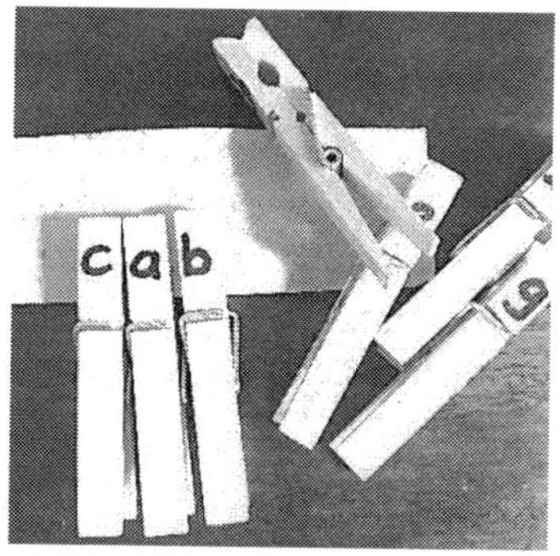

Pegs

Write graphemes onto wooden clothes pegs; the children then use the pegs to form words. They can make up their own words or copy word or picture cards. Print some picture cards with the associated words and leave out a grapheme in each word, the children can then clip the peg onto the card to fill in the missing grapheme.

Alphabet Shells

If you live near the beach, then collect some shells and write graphemes on the shells. If not, you can buy "shells" with letters printed on them. The children build words using the shells. These can be put into a sand or water tray, used for a beach theme, or used for a particular activity.

Mirror Letters

Acrylic mirror letters from Consortium are great to trace around, build words or use for displays. They can be hung in the classroom or used in the water tray.

Wool

Children form letters and words using bits of wool. Write down the word or letter for the child to copy. If the child cuts their pieces of wool, then this task also develops fine motor skills. This task is frustrating for perfectionists as the wool moves and the letters will not be perfect.

Alphabet Cones

Children build words using toy traffic cones. These are great to leave out as part of outside play or to use in a specific activity.

Squidgy Sparkle Letters

Squidgy sparkle letters are filled with glitter gel and provide a multi-sensory experience for the child. They trace over the shape of the letter with their fingers displacing the glittery liquid inside.

Bottle Top Graphemes

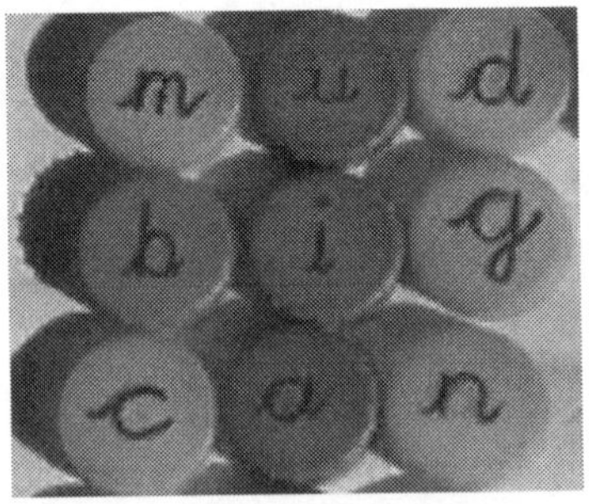

Collect milk bottle tops and write graphemes on them with a permanent marker. If you have two different coloured bottle tops, then write the vowel graphemes on one set and consonant graphemes on another. The children then use the bottle tops to make words.

Natural Items

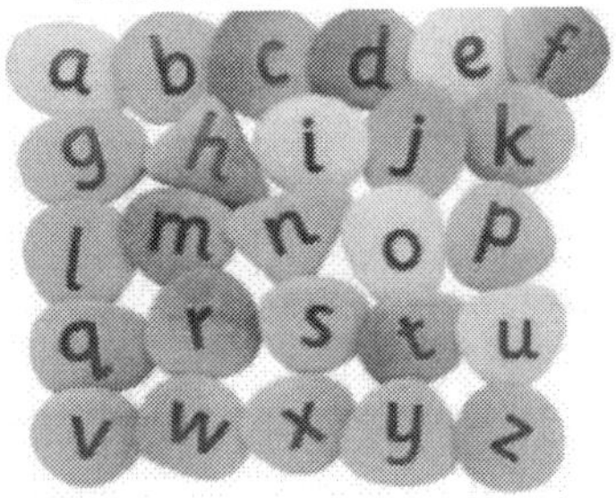

Natural items are cheap, readily available and provide children with sensory feedback. Pebbles, wood slices, sticks, acorns, and conkers are great natural items that can be used as reading manipulatives. These items can be made or bought. Write letters, graphemes, or words onto them so the children can build words or sentences.

Tactile Letters

Tactile letters are available from Consortium. They provide sensory feedback when they are traced over with a finger as they have little ridges in the shape of the letter. Children can arrange them into words or trace over them with a finger. They can use them to create words with crayon rubbing by placing the letters under a sheet of paper and gently drawing over the letter back and forth until the letter appears.

Letter Dice

Letter dice come with picture/ word cards. The dice have different letters on each side and the children use the die to form the words on the instruction cards.

Word Construction

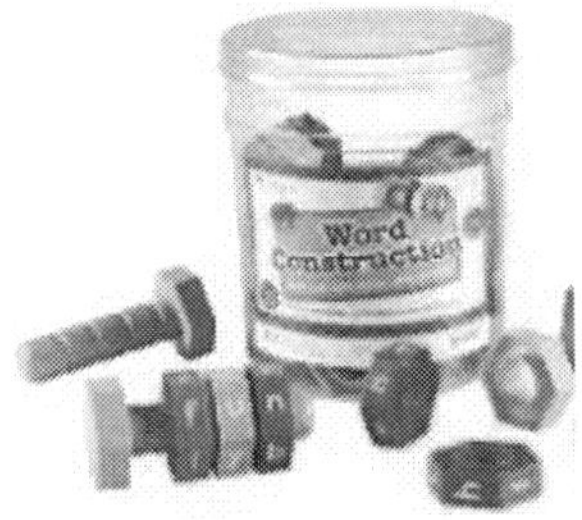

Children screw the nuts onto bolts to create words. Different sides of the bolt have different letters on them, so they can turn the nuts to make new words. This also develops fine motor control.

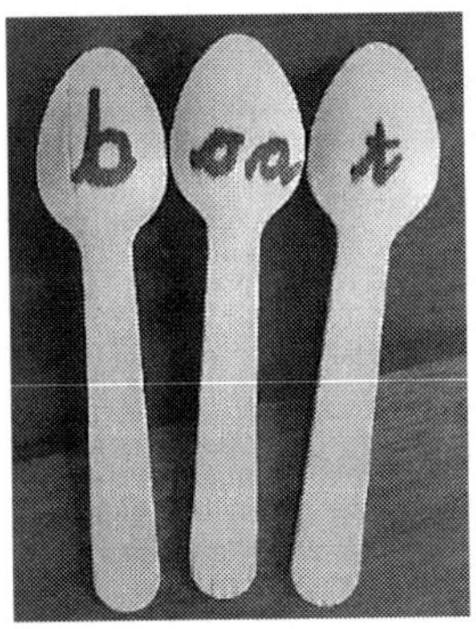

Spoon Letters

Collect any extra spoons that are left lying around after lunch and add them to your phonics resources. Write graphemes on the spoons and have the children serve up some words on a plate by placing the spoons next to each other to form words.

Mark Making

Before children start to write letters and numbers, they need lots of opportunities to develop their pre-writing skills. These activities should be fun and play based. Give children a variety of types of paper and stationery. Writing implements can be included in all play areas and writing opportunities should occur naturally throughout the day.

Drawing Development

Children learn to draw in stages. Babies make uncontrolled scribbles and vertical and horizontal lines. Toddlers use controlled scribbling to make circles, and shapes that resemble capital T's and V's. A 3-year-old draws crosses, dots, squares, and H shapes, while a 4- year-old will form triangles and diamonds.

Shape Drawing

Children need to draw a variety of shapes before learning to write. Children can copy the teacher or trace over dotted line shapes. Introduce the children to shapes in the following order:

Vertical lines

Horizontal lines

Circles

Plus signs

Forward Slash

Squares

Back Slash

Crosses

Triangles

Diamonds

Pattern Drawing

Pattern drawing develops hand strength and control. Children should draw the following patterns.

Zigzags

Wavy patterns

Polka dots

Dashes

Waves

Roller coasters

Cups

Castle turrets

Fairy doors

Bunny hops

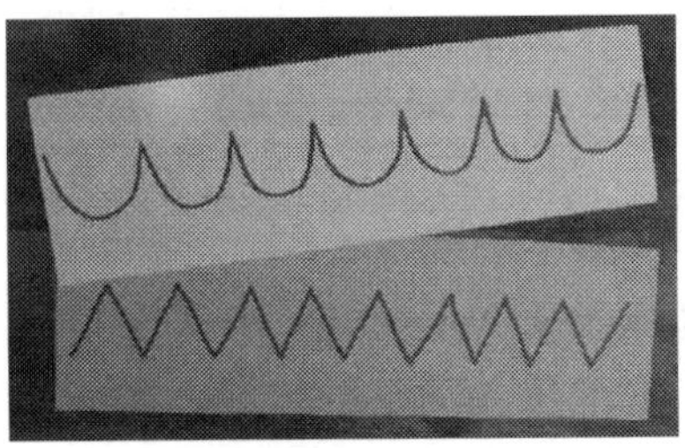

Pattern Cards

The teacher draws patterns on cards and laminates them; the children then draw over the patterns using whiteboard markers or trace the patterns using tracing paper. Children can also copy the patterns onto any of the different writing surfaces.

Pipe Cleaner Patterns

Make pattern cards by bending pipe cleaners and sticking them onto a card with PVA glue. The children then trace over the patterns using their fingers.

Mazes

Maze worksheets are great fun. Start with very simple mazes, the children find their way through the maze with a pencil. Mazes can be laminated and used annually.

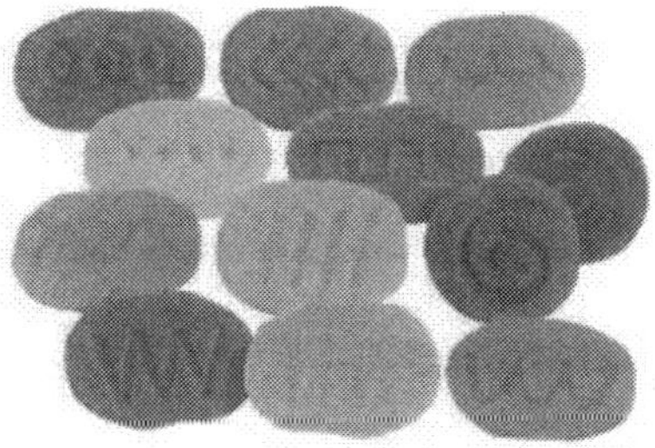

Writing Stones

Children trace over the patterns etched in the stones with their fingers. They can then they draw the prints on paper.

Pattern Roads

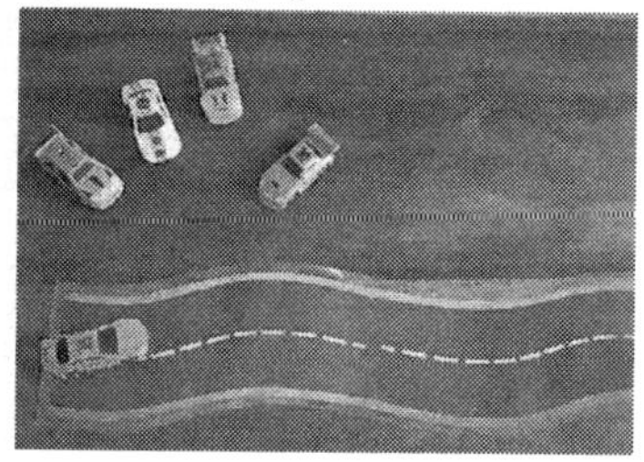

Draw or print roads in different patterns. The children then drive their cars or dry erase pens on the roads following the patterns. You could also use train tracks for this activity.

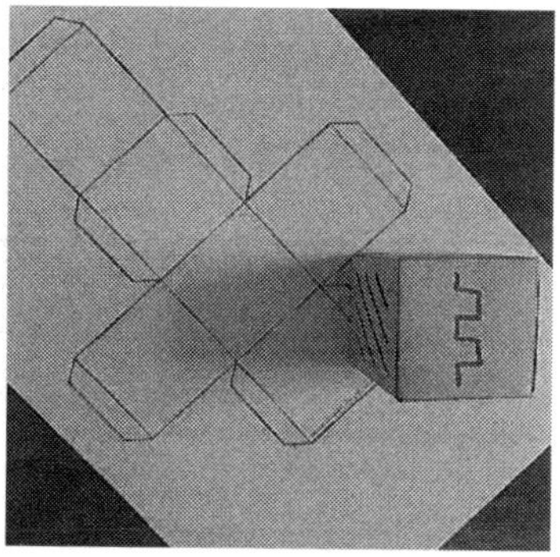

Pattern Dice

Draw writing patterns on large write-on/wipe-off dice or Insert Card Dice. Alternatively, make a dice using a cube net and draw patterns on the squares. The children then throw the dice and draw the pattern.

Funky Hair

The children use writing patterns to draw crazy hairstyles on faces or a photo of themselves. They can choose the patterns from pattern cards or dice. These pictures can make a beautiful display.

Wooden Pattern boards

Wooden pattern boards can be found on Etsy or through Montessori suppliers. The children trace the patterns on the boards using their fingers or a popsicle stick.

Name Tracing

Write the child's name on a card then paper clip tracing paper onto the name card and have the child trace their names. Do this activity daily until the child can write their name without a reference card.

17 WRITING

Letter writing

According to the Department for Education, children are not required to write in joined-up writing when they first start learning to write (2021); this supports data that suggests that some children are not yet developmentally ready to form the letters in joined-up writing at an early age. However, in my experience, it becomes difficult for some children to unlearn print and form their letters correctly using a cursive script. Print letters also lead to more letter reversals and confusion. The decision as to which script to use and when to teach it is seldom the teacher's choice and will be laid out in the school's handwriting policy.

Print Handwriting

If your school policy says to teach print letters first, then I suggest you teach the letter formation at the same time as when you learn the individual letters of the alphabet. Most phonics programmes support this order of letter formation teaching and the child will then be able to read and write the same letters.

Cursive Handwriting

Children in Reception may not be developmentally ready to write in cursive; however, when cursive handwriting is taught from the start, the children learn to write and do not need to re-learn a year or two later. If taught to write correctly, children will also never use letter reversals as it is impossible to do so when the letters are started and ended in the correct position in cursive script.

Order to Teach Cursive Handwriting

Group letters by similar form and movement and teach these letters together; this allows the child to link new knowledge to prior learning and breaks the learning into manageable chunks. I have adapted the recommendations given by occupational therapists and merged them with the letter groupings used by Sing along Handwriting. Sing-along Handwriting is my favourite way to teach handwriting, it is simple, easy to use, effective and cheap. The children learn to write letters based on a few key rhymes and hand movements. All lowercase letters start on the line. The order for teaching letter formation is:

Shooting star letters	**l, i, t, j, u, y**
Lollipop letters	**b, p, h, k**
Jelly Letters	**n, m, r**
Rainbow letters	**c, a d, g, q, o, s**
Candy cane letters	**e, f**
Ice-cream letters	**v, w**
Present letter	**z, x**

Capital Letters should be taught after lower case letters as children need lowercase letters for writing words and use capitals less often. Have an alphabet freeze in the classroom for reference purposes with the correct capital and lowercase letter formation. Capital letters always start on the top line. Teach capital letters in the following order.

A, C, O, Q, E
B, R, P, L, D
X, T, F, U, Y, V, W, M, N
G, S
I, J, H, K
Z

Top Writing Tips

For children who struggle to write on the line, use a highlighter to highlight the line in their books. Put a green sticker on the left-hand side of the page for children who forget to start on the left-hand side. For left-handed writers, write any sample letters on the right of the page so that the child can see the letter while writing.

Teaching Writing

The teacher should model each letter. The child then writes the letter several times, in the air, on the table or carpet and on their hands before writing it in their books. The teacher then moves around the classroom correcting any difficulties while the children are writing. Some children will need an example in their books to copy, while others can copy from the board. Always write examples for left-handed writers on the right-hand side of the line.

Posture for Writing

The children sit at the back of their chair, with their chairs pulled in, they sit up straight and place two feet flat on the floor. Both hands should be on the table, one hand to write and the other holds the book. Slant the paper slightly to the right for a right-handed writer and vice versa for a left-handed writer. Check left-handed, and right-handed writers are not sitting next to each other so that they do not bump their arms when they are writing.

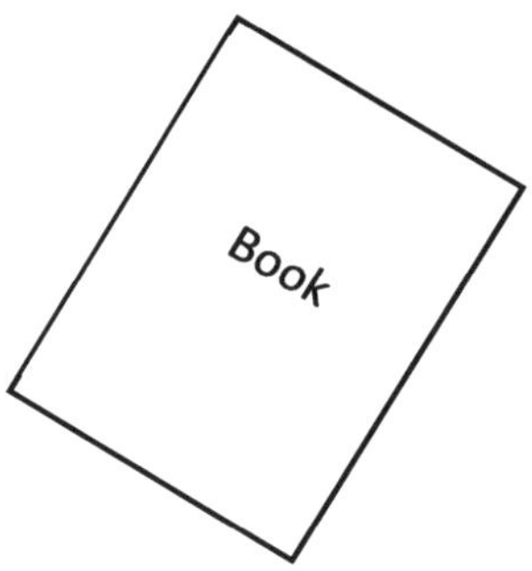

Left-Handed Writer

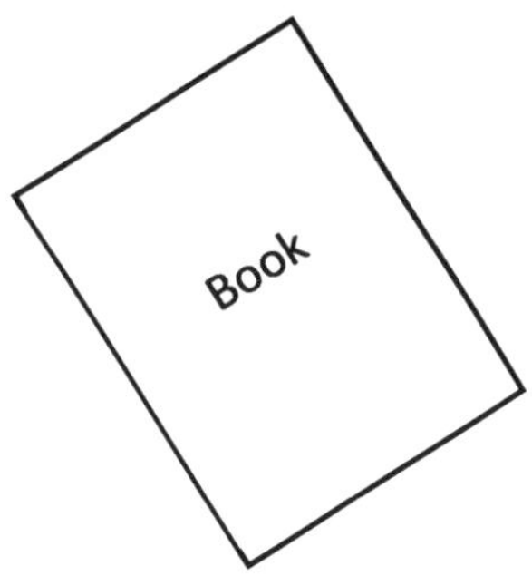

Right-Handed Writer

Tall, Tummy, Tail Letters

Children must learn the correct size and formation of letters. To do this, teach children to write on handwriting lines; these have a dotted line between the two solid lines. The child to draws a cat in the margin then uses the cat as a reference for the correct sizing of letters. Tall letters touch the top line, tummy letters touch the dotted line, and tail letters hang their tails under the line. There are a few exceptions, but children quickly learn these.

Tall Letters	**b, d, h, k, l**
Tummy Letters	**a, c, e, i, m, n, o, r, s, u, v, w, x, z**
Tail Letters	**g, j, p, q, y**
Exceptions	**t, f**

Warm-Up for Writing

Warm up the children's gross and fine motor muscles before writing lessons. The best way to do this is to make large full-body motions that imitate the hand movements needed for the family of letters you will teach in that lesson. For example, for rainbow letters, the teacher asks the children to start on the floor and make a giant rainbow using their arms, then stop and curl back round to the floor and flick back up. They can do this with both arms and then with each arm individually while crossing over the midline. Give children doweling rods with ribbons attached; they use these as magic wands and wave their Magic Writing Wands in the air to form letters.

Once the children have done a few gross motor exercises, they can then do some fine-motor exercises before writing. The children squeeze and stretch their fingers a few times, flick their fingers or place their hands flat on the table and raise each finger in turn.

Handwriting Whiteboard

Make or buy cursive handwriting charts. The children can practice writing letters on the boards using dry erase markers every day.

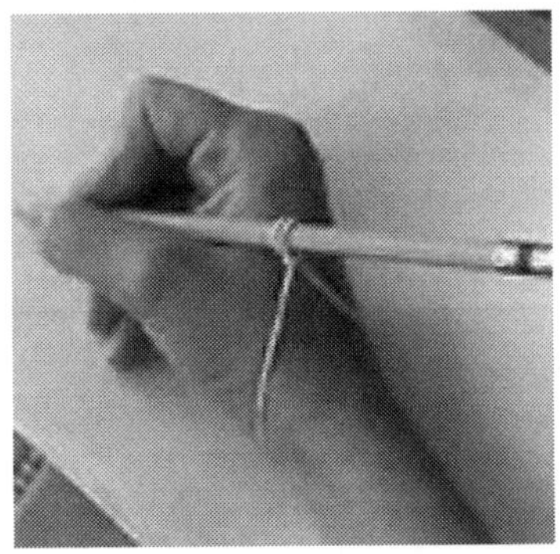

Pencil Grip

There are a range of pencil grips available online to help children who struggle with poor pencil grip. Have the child try various pencil grips and choose the one the child likes the most. Alternatively, loop an elastic around the pencil and the child's hand to keep the pencil in the correct position, ensure the elastic is not too tight.

Left-Handed Writers

Left-handed children should be given pencils with the grooves in the correct position for left-handed writers. These children should use left-handed scissors as the blade is in a different position making cutting easier. Any example letters or patterns should be on the right-hand side of the page. Where possible, have a left-handed teacher or teaching assistant demonstrate fine motor skills for these children to avoid confusion.

Letter Stones

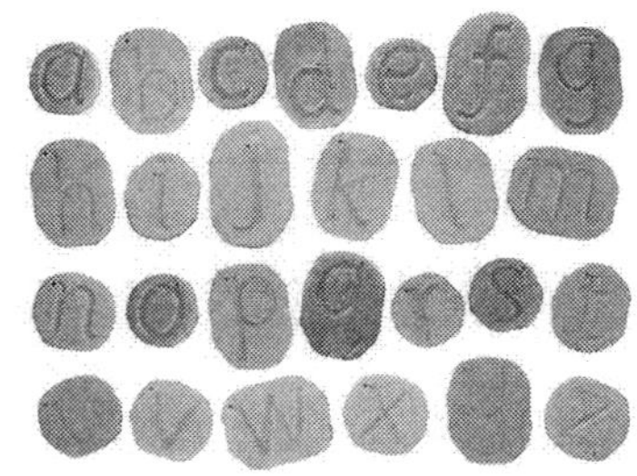

Children trace over letters etched into stone with their fingers. They start the letter on the green dot so that they also learn the correct letter formation.

Magnetic Learning Letters

These Magnetic Learning Letters are a Montessori resource. The children trace over letters using the stick provided or a finger; this helps build the mental image of the letter's shape and build muscle memory.

Wooden Handwriting Board

You can have wooden handwriting boards made with the script of your choice on Etsy. The children trace over the letters etched into a wooden handwriting board with a finger or a lollipop stick. By doing these actions, they build up muscle memory and a mental image of the letter. The child can also fill the letters with seeds or pebbles to build in a sensory element to the learning activity.

Sandpaper Letters

Cut out lowercase letters in sandpaper. The child then traces over the letters with their fingers. Put a dot on the starting and ending position on the letter. Show the child how to form the letter and then let the child use their finger to write over the letter. You can also buy sandpaper letters from Montessori supplies, as always check that the font is the same as the one you use in your school.

Flashcards

Go through the grapheme flashcards every day. Have a child choose a flashcard and then write the letter on their whiteboards.

Letter Roads

Make and print roads for toy cars in the shape of letters. The children then drive toy cars on the roads as if they were writing the letters. Ensure they start and end in the correct place. They could also write or paint the letters on the roads. Twinkl have a great selection of writing roads in a variety of handwriting fonts.

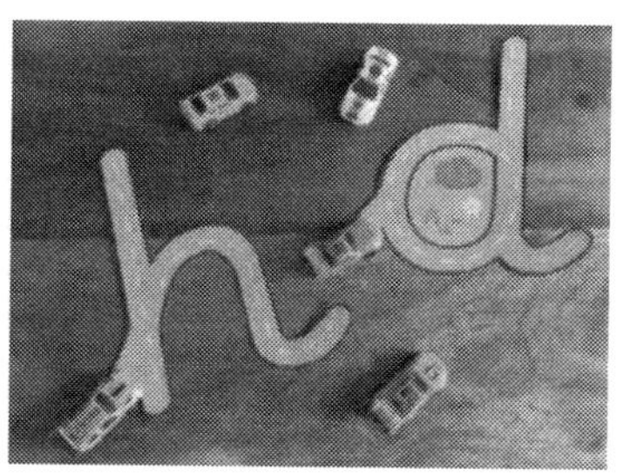

Alphabet Strip

It takes time for children to learn the correct letter formation for each letter. A strip with the correct script in alphabetical order can be printed and attached to the table for the child to refer to when writing.

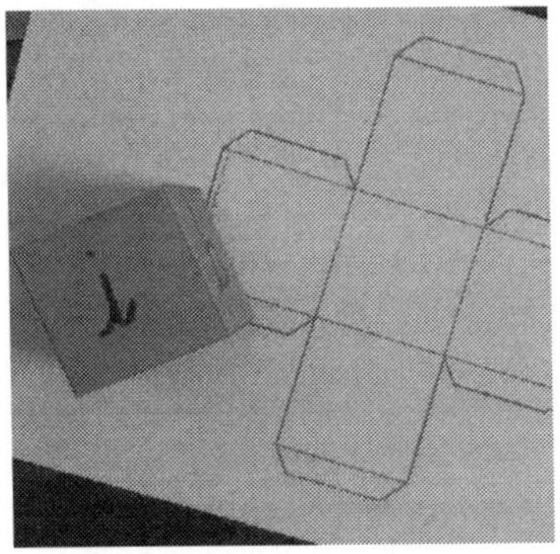

Alphabet Dice

Make die from a cube net and write a few letters on the die. The child throws the dice and then practices writing the letter. They can do this in groups or independently.

Letter Tracing

Write letters on instruction cards and laminate them so they can be used again. Then paperclip tracing paper or greaseproof baking paper over the card. The child then traces over the letter.

Sing-Along Handwriting

A great app to support the teaching and learning of handwriting is Sing-along Handwriting. This app costs a few pounds and has catchy rhymes to support children in learning the formation of letters. You can mirror an iPad or tablet so that the children can see the app on screen for whole-class instruction. Children enjoy the rhymes, and their handwriting noticeably improves with this app. I often recommend this app to parents as it is inexpensive, and children can practise handwriting at home without any specialised instruction or supervision.

Nelson Handwriting Programme

Nelson Handwriting is a handwriting course that can be used from Reception through to Year Six, ensuring a consistent approach to handwriting throughout the school. I have visited many schools and have found that the schools that use the Nelson Handwriting Books have children with the best handwriting.

Nelson

Handwriting

Word Writing

Teach word writing in as many ways as possible; this keeps the learning fresh and exciting, but it also gives learners with varying styles of learning opportunities to learn.

Sound Tap

Sound tap is a kinaesthetic method of learning, say a word, the child then taps out the sounds in the word on the table. Starting at the pinkie the child taps one finger on the table for each sound. The child can have a picture of a hand on their table to remind them of how to tap out sounds when they first learn this exercise. Once they have tapped the sounds, they then write the sounds to make the word.

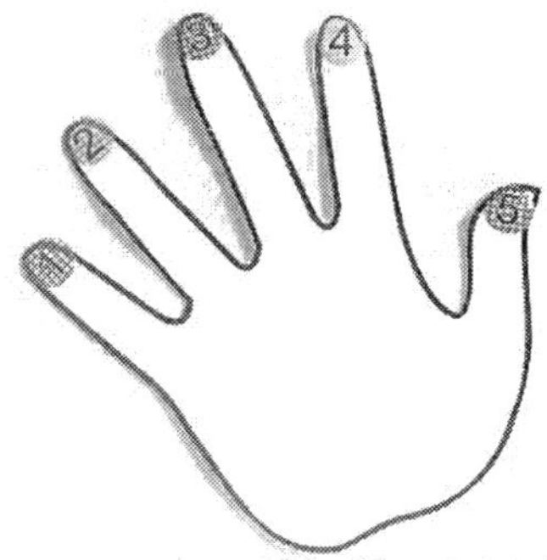

Trip, t (Tap pinkie on the table)
r (Tap ring finger)
i (Tap middle finger)
p (Tap pointer)
Write **trip**

Group Writing

Give a group of children a word. They then sound out the word, and each child writes one of the sounds on their whiteboard. The children then hold their whiteboards and arrange themselves so that the word is in order and the rest of the class can read their word.

Phoneme Frames

Children are given pictures of decodable words on cards with phoneme frames. They use magnetic letters to make the words. The phoneme frames are the same shape as the word. They then move each grapheme out of the frame boxes and write in the grapheme. Phoneme frames are helpful when teaching digraphs as the child must make or write the sounds in each box and begin to see the digraphs as units of sound.

Sound Trains

Sound trains are a fun way to present phoneme frames. Print and laminate a train with train cars. Each car on the train holds a sound. The children then pick a picture card, sound out the word and put the sounds on the train.

Phoneme Strips

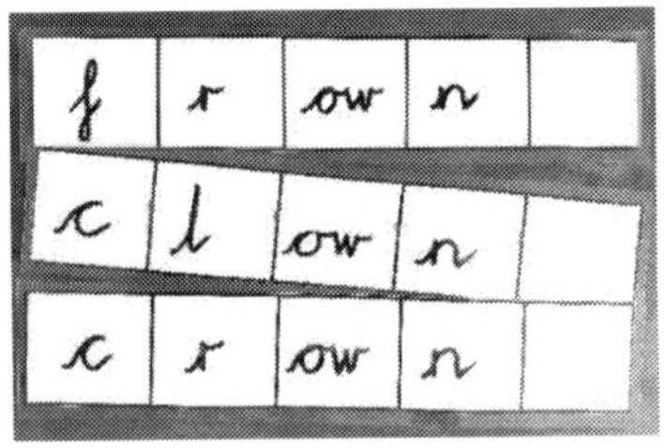

Each child gets a phoneme strip. Say a word, and the child places magnetic letters on the phoneme frame or write the graphemes into the phoneme frames. Each box on the frame holds one sound (not necessarily a letter) as some boxes will hold more letters as they may hold digraphs or trigraphs. It is important children understand that not every box will need a sound as shorter words will have fewer sounds. Phoneme frames can be used to sound out any decodable word.

Magnetic Letter Word building

Give the child a set of letter cards or magnetic letters. Say a word and have them make the word with the letters. They need to say the word, say the sounds, count the sounds and then make the word and read the word; this can also be an independent activity if you give the child a set of picture cards; they then make the word with the letters. Later, children can write the word.

Word Ladders

Part of learning to spell is learning to have fun with language. A word ladder is a great way to do this. Give the child one word; four-letter words work best for this activity; they re-write the word underneath, changing only one letter to create a new word. They repeat the task until they cannot make a new word. The words must all be real words.

tent
tend
bend
send
lend
lent

This game can also be played with more specific instructions, such as they can only change the last or first letter; this develops a greater understanding of the structure of words.

Rhyming Word Chains

Give the child one word, and they think of as many rhyming words as they can; these can be real or nonsense words. The children write these on strips of paper and join them to make a chain to hang up in the classroom.

Roll a Word

Children use grapheme dice to create words; this game can be played in small groups or independently.

Tri-blocks

Graphemes are printed on triangular prism blocks; children build words using Tri-Blocks. The vowels and consonants are in different colours so that children learn through experience that words need both.

Mini Chalkboards

Mini Chalkboards are great for sounding out and writing words. Give the child a picture or say the word. The child sounds out the word and counts the sound. They then take out the required number of chalkboards, write the sounds on the chalkboards and place them in order. There should be one chalkboard per phoneme and not per letter. Mini Chalkboards can be found online, in Poundland or you can make your own with blackboard paint.

Letter, Word, or Sentence?

Say a word, a letter, or a sentence. The children must identify if it is a letter, word, or sentence; this develops an understanding of the different concepts and helps with spelling and sentence writing.
Teacher: Is this a letter, a word, or a sentence?
d (say the letter name, not the sound)
Children: letter
Teacher: Is this a letter, a word, or a sentence?
She went to the shops.
Children: sentence
Teacher: Is this a letter, a word, or a sentence?
fish
Children: word

CVCC Magnetic Words

Tell the child a CVC word, and they make it using magnetic letters. Then ask the child to add one letter to the word to create a new word.
Teacher: Make the word **hum**.
Child: **hum**.
Teacher: Add one letter to your word to make the word **hump**.
Child: **h-u-m-p**, **hump**.

CVCC Whiteboard Words

Say a CVC word, and the children write it on their whiteboards. Then expand the word into a CVCC word and repeat it. Then ask the children what the difference is between the two words. The children point out the ending sound and add a letter onto their word on their whiteboards.

Teacher: Write the word **men.**

Children: **m-e-n, men.**

Teacher: If I say the words **men** and **mend**, what do you notice?

Children: **Mend** has a **d** sound on the end of the word.

Teacher: That is right, let us write the word **mend**.

ten-tent	men-mend	hum-hump	ben-bent	ben-bend
dam-damp	ram-pram	lug-plug	rum-drum	den-dent
win-wind	ban-band	pan-pant	ban-bank	pen-pent

CCVC Magnetic Words

Tell the child a CVC word, and they make it using magnetic letters. Then ask the child to add one letter to the word to create a new word.

Teacher: Make the word **win.**

Child: **win.**

Teacher: Add one letter to your word to make the word **win.**

Child: **t-w-i-n, twin.**

CCVC Whiteboard Words

Say a CVC word, and the children write it on their whiteboards. Then expand the word into a CCVC word and repeat it. Then ask the children what the difference is between the two words. The children point out the initial sound **s** and complete their words on their whiteboards.

Teacher: Write the word **pin.**

Children: **p-i-n, pin.**

Teacher: If I say the words **pin** and **spin**, what do you notice?

Children: **Spin** has an **i** sound at the beginning.

Teacher: That is right, let us write the word **spin.**

pot-spot	pin-spin	peck-speck	win-twin	top stop
lap-clap	lad-glad	ran-gran	rip-grip	cab-scab
lap-slap	wig-twig	nip-snip	pun-spun	pit-spit

Sentence Writing

Learning to write a sentence is a long process. If a child starts to struggle at any point in the process, go back one step, find where the child is having difficulties, do some intervention and then move on. The ability to write a good sentence is essential for all other writing, so ensure the child has a solid foundation in sentence writing.

Sentence Writing

Show the children a simple picture, then demonstrate how to think of a sentence, say the sentence, count the words in the sentence, write the sentence, and then check the sentence. Demonstrate how to use a capital letter at the beginning of a sentence and a full stop at the end but do not emphasise the punctuation at this point as the child has a lot to remember when they start to write sentences. Children can use sound charts to help them identify the sounds in words. Repeat this modelling process often until children fully understand and use this method for writing sentences.
I am going to **think** of a sentence:
Sit on a rock.
Let me **count** how many words:
Sit on a rock—four (hold up four fingers).
Now I am going to **write** the sentence:
S-i-t o-n a r-o-ck.
Let me **check** my sentence:
Sit on a rock.

Sentence Snipping

The child says a sentence, then you write the sentence and the child cuts between the words and sticks the sentence in order. The child can then re-write the sentence underneath.

Word Rearranging

Print a picture and a set of words that create a sentence. The child arranges the words into a logical sentence and then write the sentence. Put a capital letter on the first word and a full stop next to the last word to help early writers and readers rearrange the words correctly.

fish	The	happy.	is

Cube writing

The child says the sentence they want to write and counts the words in the sentence. They then count out the same number of cubes and join them together; they then refer to the cubes as they write the sentence to help them keep track of the words in their sentence. This kinaesthetic approach to writing helps children remember all the words in their sentence.

Sentence Opener Cards

Print words that can be used to start sentences. The children choose a sentence starter and then use it to write a sentence. Use a capital letter at the beginning of sentence openers to ensure children use this when writing a sentence.

Some good sentence openers are:

Next	Then	When	Lastly
I	He	She	They
As	Once	First	Second

Sentence Starters

Choose simple phrases or words that can be used to begin sentences and leave out the last word and ensure that the word must be a noun. Create picture cards of decodable words that can be substituted at the end of the sentences. The children write the sentence and sound out and write the word for the picture. They then repeat the sentence using a different card. This activity gives reluctant writers the confidence to write. The phrase "I can see a" is not a good sentence starter to teach as children who learn to write this phrase tend to get stuck on it and find it difficult to think of other ideas to write when they write independently.

Some good sentence starters are:

He fed the
She has a
They like
He sat on the
I go to the
I like
She went to the
The dog ran after the

Group Writing

Children compose a sentence as a group. Each child writes one of the words in the sentence on a whiteboard. They then arrange the words into the right order and hold up their whiteboards for the rest of the class to read. The rest of the class can suggest ways to improve the sentence, like using a capital letter, full stop or the addition of adjectives or adverbs.

Talk for Writing

Talk for writing is a method used to teach writing that Pie Corbett pioneered. The children learn a story as a class and then retell that story with actions, a story map, props, or a combination of these memory aids. Once they are confident in telling the story, they then write the story. The children can then be encouraged to innovate the story by changing the setting, characters, or problem. This method of teaching writing is very effective as children know what they are going to write before they start.

Post-It Sentences

The child thinks of a sentence, then writes each word on a separate post-it note and sticks the words on their desk in order. If they are working with a partner or in a group, then the other child can read the sentence and check it for capital letters, full stops and to ensure it makes sense. These sentences can be re-written in their books, or you can take a photograph as evidence.

Mighty Writer

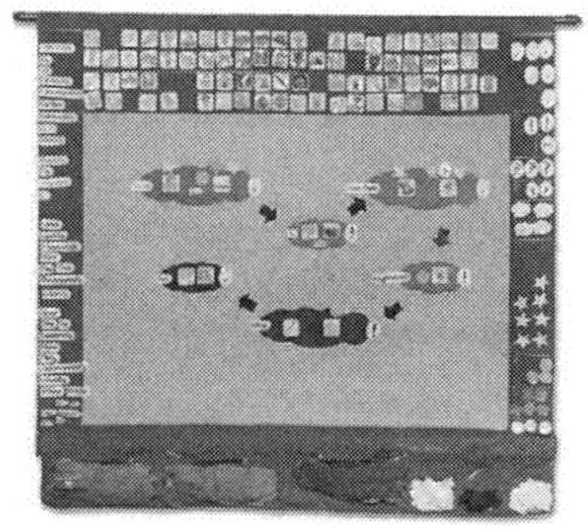

The Mighty Writer is a learning resource for classrooms that uses visual aids to assist children in better understanding the concept of a sentence. There are pictures for nouns, sentence openers, punctuation, and symbols for adjectives, adverbs, and verbs. Sentences are then visually composed on a sentence bubble—green bubbles for the beginning, orange for the middle and red for the end of a paragraph or story. Children make the sentence using the Mighty Writer, and then they use those bubbles to write their sentence.

Mighty Writer helps children structure their writing and helps struggling writers retain their ideas. It can be used for whole class or small group teaching and is a good resource for writing interventions. I am a huge fan of Mighty Writer for Reception and Year One and saw a marked improvement in my classes' writing.

Silly Sentences

Give the children a table with the parts of sentences in separate columns. They use these sentence components to compose silly sentences and then write the sentences. These sentences can also be printed onto different coloured card, and the children can make them using the card and then write the sentences.

Sentence Starter	Adjective		Noun		Verb		Prepositional Phrase	
The	huge	red	elephant	wizard	eats	giggles	in the ocean.	to the shops.
My	blue	silver	unicorn	dinosaur	runs	frowns	through the air.	around the world.
A	angry	fluffy	fairy	tiger	hops	flies	to the castle	under the table.
An	happy	spiky	monster	lion	cooks	stomps	during the show.	in my head.
Her	pretty	slimy	dragon	clown	bakes	swims	at school.	on my head.
His	scary	tiny	mermaid	teacher	sweeps	roars	into the house.	over the city.
Their	hungry	invisible	knight	ghost	writes	whispers	out of the tower.	into space.
Our	beautiful	friendly	princess	monkey	jumps	paints	into a cave	to the moon.
Your	green	clever	witch	alien	skips	draws	away from danger	to a friend.

Stretch A Sentence

Say a simple sentence, the children write the sentence on a whiteboard. Then use question words to have the children expand on the sentence. With each question, the children should amend or re-write their sentence. The aim is not for every sentence to be written like this but rather to enrich their writing. You may only focus on one or two of the questions if you want to teach a particular element of a sentence.

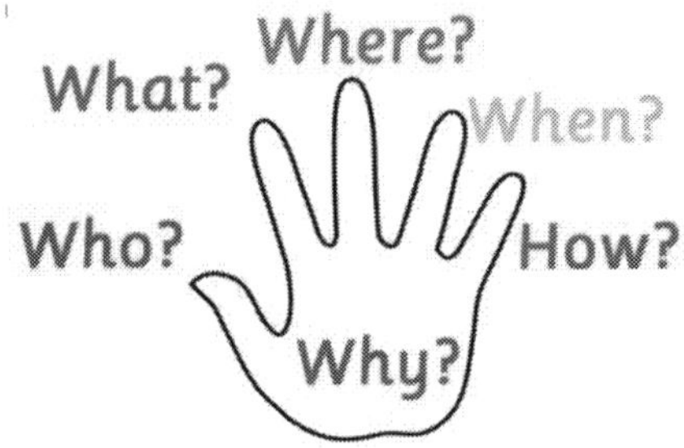

Teacher: The man went fishing.
Teacher: **Who** went fishing? Describe him to me.
Children: The **old** man went fishing.
Teacher: **What** was he fishing for?
Children: The old man went fishing for **sharks**.
Teacher: **Where** did he go fishing?
Children: The old man went fishing for sharks in the **Pacific Ocean**.
Teacher: **When** did he go fishing?
Children: The old man went fishing for sharks in the Pacific Ocean **at night.**
Teacher: **How** did he fish for sharks?
Children: The old man **brazenly** went fishing for sharks in the Pacific Ocean at night.
Teacher: **Why** did he go fishing for sharks?
Children: The old man brazenly went fishing for sharks in the Pacific Ocean at night **because he wanted to make shark soup**.
Teacher: Is there **anything else** we could do to make our sentence more interesting?
Children: The old man brazenly went fishing for sharks in the Pacific Ocean at night because he wanted to make shark soup **for his wedding**.

Independent Writing

It is imperative to model sentence writing when children are first learning to write; this can be done on the board or with a visualiser or on a clipboard with small groups. Children should be encouraged to follow the steps for every sentence they write, this may seem laboured, but it is better to have one or two good sentences than a page full of random letters and words. For every sentence, the child should:

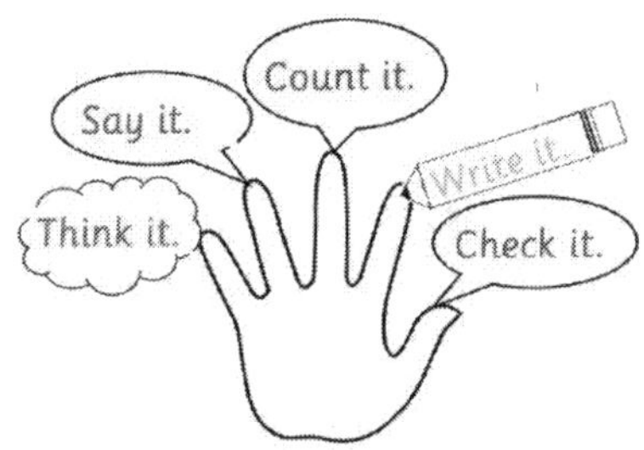

Think of a sentence.
Say the sentence (to a partner or their pencil).
Count the words (repeat the sentence out loud while counting the words).
Write the sentence.
Check the sentence (the child reads the sentence out loud and checks that there is a capital letter, full stop, finger spaces between words and if the sentence makes sense).
The children can check they have completed all the steps by going through the steps on a hand while saying: think it (first finger), say it (second finger), count it (third finger), write it (fourth finger), check it (last finger).

Writing Activities

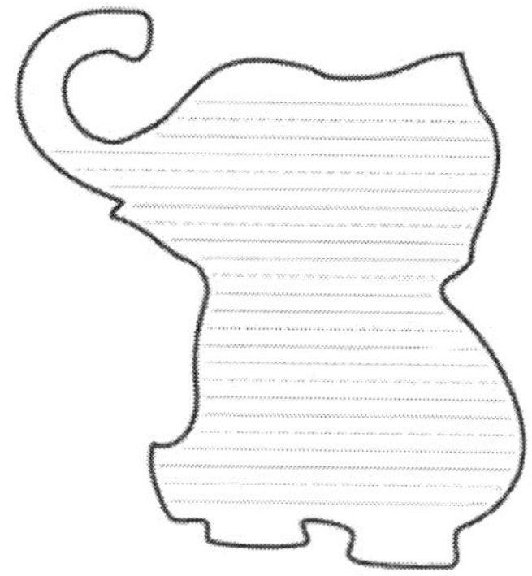

Writing is hard work and children are easily discouraged so it is important to make the activity as interesting as possible. Provide them with as many different types of writing activities, use writing frames, interesting paper, and real-world objects to get children excited about their writing. Muse Printables has a huge variety of fun writing templates.

Here is a short list of some possible writing activities:
Words-spelling words, Common Exception words, word families or subject specific words.
Captions- short phrases usually without punctuation for early writers.
Sentences- fiction and non-fiction.
Paragraphs- fiction and non-fiction about a range of topics.
Narratives- traditional tales, writing based on a text, morality tales.
Poetry- rhyming poems, acronyms, shape poems, spoonerisms.
Diaries/ Journals/Blogs-historical figures (Samuel Pepys, Robert Scott), diary entries for book characters, their own diary entries. A journal provides more scope for creativity and a blog is a more modern alternative to a diary.
Letters- Get involved in the Flat Stanley project (register your school online) and send real letters to other children in other schools around the world. Or write a letter to a family member, pen pals, a character in a story, Father Christmas, the Tooth Fairy, the Queen, or the Prime Minister.
Envelopes- address real envelopes for your letters, these can be stuck in their books, or the letters can be sent.
Postcards- from a book character, or a country you have been learning about.
Cards-birthday, thank you, Christmas, Easter, and get-well cards.
Invitations-birthday, wedding, and graduation.
Recipes-real or nonsense.
Instructions- for something the children can do well such as brushing their teeth.
Recipes-these can be fun recipes with silly ingredients like Roald Dahl's Georges Marvellous Medicine or it can be the recipe for something you are making in class.
Book/Film reviews- these provide an opportunity for persuasive writing.
Fact Files- these can be linked with Geography or Science.
Autobiographies- they can write their own autobiography or pretend to be an historical figure.
Biographies- write about an important historical figure.
Plays or scripts- Nativity play, YouTube Script, or animation script.
Posters- wanted poster, information poster, persuasive poster, shop poster.
E-mails/texts- these can be part of a computing lesson and children can send you an email.
Comics- superheroes or their own comic about a story or an event.
Experiments- have children write the experiments you do in science.
Shape Writing-write into the shape of an object to motivate children in their writing.

18 SPELLING

Good spellers can hear the sounds in words and then write the correct graphemes or say those graphemes using the letter names. It is therefore important to teach children to say the letter names as there is a difference between sounding out a word and spelling a word. The first few activities focus on learning the alphabet, all the activities after that can be used to help children learn their spelling words

The Alphabet

Children should learn to say and order the alphabet using the letter names. Avoid singing the alphabet as children let the letters run into each other and do not learn the alphabet correctly. To learn the alphabet, they can say it, write it in order or alphabetise letter manipulatives. Higher attaining pupils can alphabetise words by their first letter and then later by their second and third letters.

Alphabet Letter Sorting

The children sort magnetic letters into the alphabet. They can sort lowercase or uppercase letters or both.

Alphabet Sorting

Print out lowercase letter cards with pictures on them. The children arrange the letters in alphabetical order. Later the children can arrange lowercase letter cards without pictures and then capital letter cards.

Matching capital to lowercase

The children match lowercase letters to capital letters. Start with a few letters and then work up to all the letters in the alphabet.

Fancy Stuff Spelling

Children write their spelling words in fancy writing, spooky writing, or bubble writing. They can then decorate and colour their words. The more time they take, colours they use, and fun they have, the more likely children will remember their words.

Smart Snacks Alpha Pops

The children link the capital letter with the lowercase letter. These pops are self-correcting as the colours help the children find the correct letters.

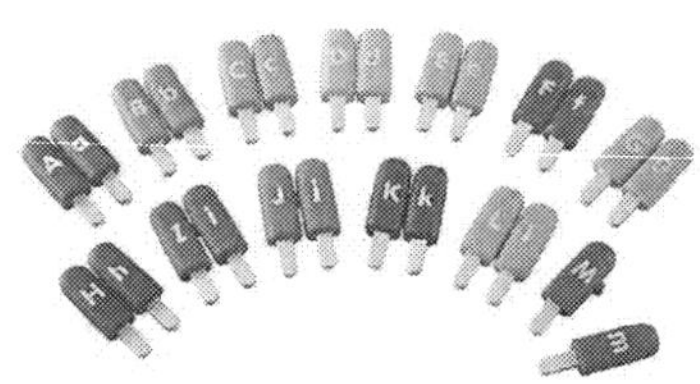

Sound chart

Children use sound charts as a reference material when they are sounding out unfamiliar words on their own. They think of a word, then break the word into sounds, they write down the graphemes they know and look up the phoneme they are unsure of on the sound chart and pick the grapheme that looks the most correct to them. You can make your own sound charts, download them from Twinkl or buy them from Jolly Phonics or THRASS. The best sound charts I have ever worked with are the THRASS charts which can be purchased with a matching classroom frieze.

Spelling PLAIT

A spelling PLAIT is two-sided sound chart designed to help struggling spellers decide on the correct grapheme. One side is for consonant sounds and one side is for vowel sounds. Children use a spelling PLAIT in a similar way to a sound chart. They look for the sounds they want to use and then write them down. The benefit of a spelling PLAIT is that children are not overwhelmed by visual information. The child can only see one sound at a time; all the other sounds are greyed out; they can then choose to see the alternate graphemes for that sound or keep them covered and look at the most common spelling choice. This multi-sensory resource is beneficial for children with visual processing difficulties and Dyslexia

Hangman

Traditional hangman is not appropriate for small children, but you can play the same game using a stick figure or a flower. Every time they make an incorrect guess, a body part is rubbed out until the stickman or flower becomes invisible. To make it a bit more predictable, play hangman with the Tricky Words, Common Exception Words or High-Frequency Words.

Digraph Flowers

Give each child or group a circle with a digraph written on it. They then think of as many different words as they can with that digraph. They write each word on oval pieces of coloured paper to make petals and stick them around the circle to create a flower. The flowers can then be used as part of a display or on the spelling wall.

Sound Family Turkeys

Decorate paper cups to look like turkeys and label them with different graphemes from the same sound family. Write words from the same sound family but with alternate spellings on lollipop sticks. Place all the sticks upside down on the table. Each child picks a stick and then posts it in the right turkey cup to create its' tail.

Mini Whiteboard cards

Create mini whiteboards by laminating plain paper and cutting it into squares. Give the child a word; they read the word, sound it out, count the number of phonemes and get the same number of mini white whiteboards. They then write each sound on a mini whiteboard and arrange the whiteboards to form the word.

Build, Cover, Spell

Give the child a list of words to practice. They build each word with manipulatives such as magnetic letters and then covers it and write the word.

Look, Say, Cover, Write, Check

Give the child a list of words. They look at the word, say the word, cover the word, write it, and lastly, check that they have spelt it correctly. This method only works for children with a strong visual memory.

Look, Say, Cover, Write, Check

Look, say, cover	Write	Check
bomb		
climb		
comb		
crumb		
dumb		
lamb		
limb		
numb		
plumbing		
thumb		

Read, sound, write, check

Read, sound, write, check is a good method for children to use when learning their spelling as they can recall the knowledge later. Print the spelling words in a list down the left-hand side of the page. The child reads each word, sounds it out and places sound buttons or dashes under each grapheme (use a dot for graph and a dash for digraphs or trigraphs). The child then writes the words in the second column (with the first column still visible), sounding them out as they write them. The child then folds the page to cover the words and writes the word in the third column. They then open the flap and check their spelling. If they get the word right, they put a tick in the last column; if they made a mistake, they write the word correctly in the last column.

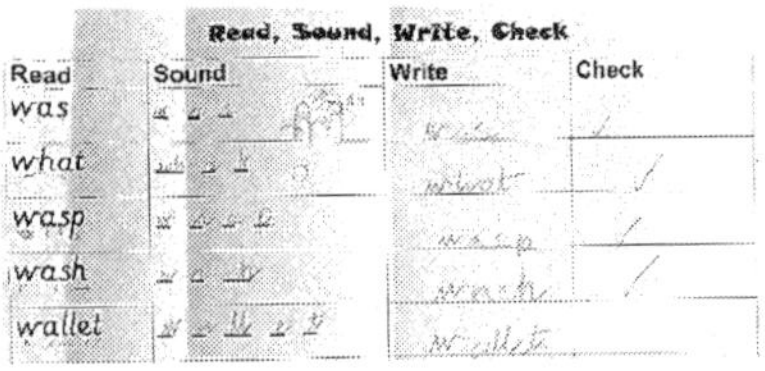

Trace, Write, Draw and Make

Create a table with four columns. In the first column type, the words in the font the children use in class. The children then trace over each typed word, re-write the word in the second column, draw a picture representing the word in the third column and then use alphabet stickers to make the word in the last column. I always put the sticker activity last as the children love stickers, so they make good incentives to complete the other activities.

Trace, Write, Draw & Make

Trace	Write	Draw	Make
old			
cold			
gold			
hold			
told			
most			
only			
both			
whole			

Sound Family

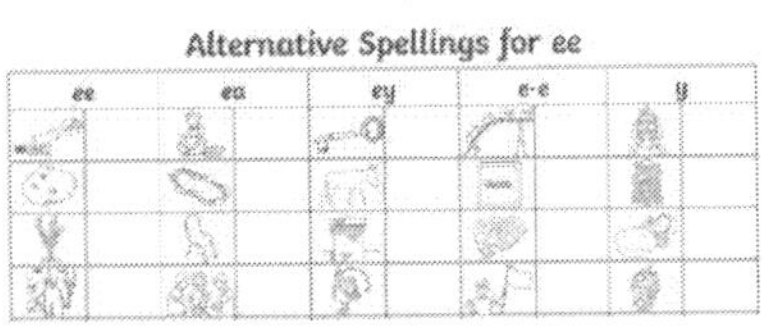

Create a table for each sound family, the different graphemes for the phoneme are used as column headers. Insert pictures into the table; the child spells the word for each image using the grapheme in the column heading. Twinkl has ready-made sound family mats.

Phoneme Spotter Sort

Print or type a Phoneme Spotter (a text with words from the same sound family). The child reads the text and finds all the words from the target sound, highlights them, and then writes them on post-its or sorts them into tables according to their graphemes.

ai Sound Family Phoneme Spotter Story

Sid the Snail

Sid was fed up with being just a snail and decided he wanted to try something new. One day during the month of May he decided to become a weather reporter. He crawled outside leaving a slimy trail behind him. At first it was warm and sunny and he liked being outdoors, but soon the grey clouds came and it began to rain. Just then it started to hail and Sid had to quickly hide inside his shell, where he felt safe. He didn't want to be a weather reporter anymore!

Rhyming Chains

Children write words that rhyme on strips of paper. They then join the strips to create a chain. The chains can be joined and put up around the classroom.

Rainbow Writing

Give the child a list of words. They write each word using crayons or colouring pencils. For each word they write over it again and again with different colours creating a rainbow effect. Children will learn to spell the words through repetition and the use of colour.

Active Spelling

Each child has a ball; you call out a word, and the children spell the word as they bounce their ball. Children who are still learning to spell can say the sounds, middle ability children can say the sounds and the letter names while proficient spellers can say the letter names.

Crack and Spell

Hide the letters for a word inside a plastic egg. The child opens the egg and rearranges the letters to make a word. They can then write the word, put the pieces back into the egg and pass it to a friend while taking another egg.

Changing Words

Changing words is a great game when children are learning about rhyme. Place a word ending on the table like **at**, the children then place or write various letters at the front of the word ending to make new words like **cat, rat, mat, pat** and **fat**.

Syllabification

Teach children to break words into syllables by clapping the rhythm of the word. They can then spell out each section of the word; each syllable will have a vowel sound. Syllabification is also important for several spelling rules in Year Two.
yesterday can be split into **yes/ter/day**

Word Families

Word families are groups of words that follow the same spelling conventions. When children begin seeing word families, it is easier for them to learn to spell as they only need to learn to spell one or two words and then use the same rule to spell the rest. When teaching spelling words, it is best to teach them in word families as repetition aids retainment.

Pyramid Writing

The child writes the first letter of a word on the first line, then underneath, they write the first and second letter and underneath that, they write the first three letters until the word is complete. They can then turn their word into a pyramid or a sailing boat.

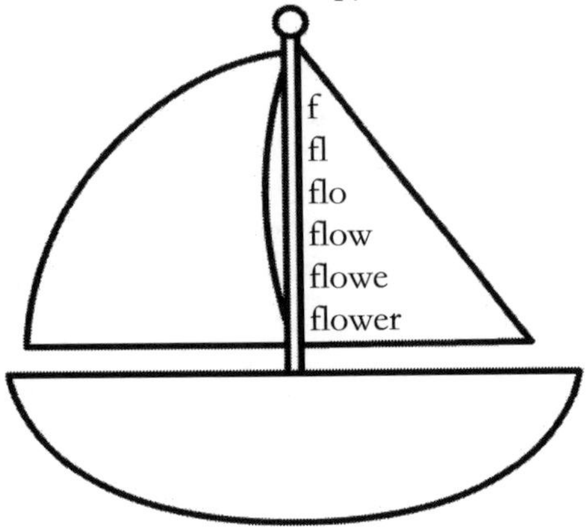

Interactive Board Games

There are many great interactive games available some are free, and others are paid, or subscription based. *Phonics Play* has both free and paid games. *Jolly Phonics* has interactive software that can be loaded onto the computer, and *Twinkl* also has some interactive games.

Take Your Pencil for A Walk

The child places their pencil on the page; they then keep the pencil down and "walk" all around the page using the pencil. When they are finished, they write their spelling words into their doodle.

Tap and Spell

Say a word, the child sounds out the word whilst tapping the sounds out onto the table starting with the pinkie. Print a hand to remind learners when they are still learning this technique.

Teacher: **Ship**.
Child: **sh** (tap the pinkie on the table)
i (tap the ring finger)
p (tap the middle finger)
Ship (Child writes the word).

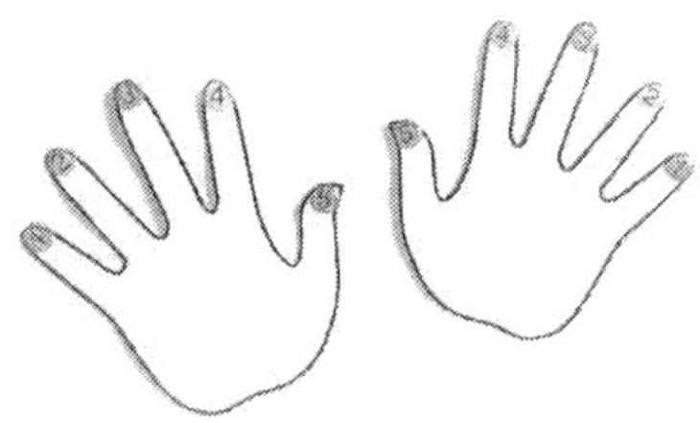

Tap and Clap

Say a word, the child then sounds out the word whilst tapping their thumb to a finger for every sound. They blend the word and clap as they say the word.

Teacher: **Train**.
Child: **t** (thumb to pinkie),
r (thumb to ring finger),
ai (thumb to middle finger)
n (thumb to pointer).
Train (Child claps as they say the word).

Hourglass Writing

The child writes the word; they then write it again underneath, leaving out the last letter. They then leave out each subsequent letter until only the initial letter is left and then add each letter until the word is complete.

writer
write
writ
wri
wr
w
wr
wri
writ
write
writer

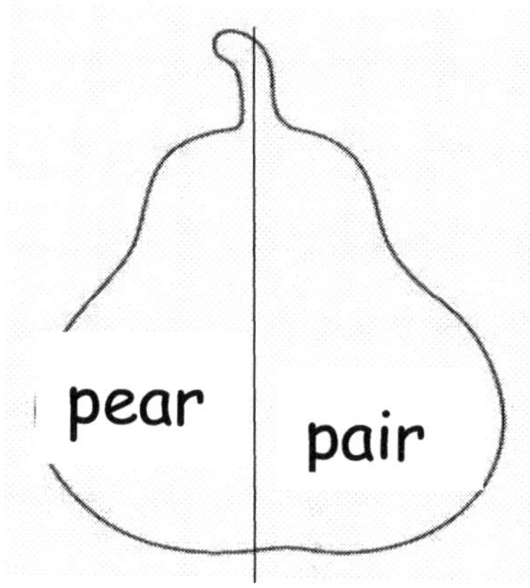

Homophone Pears

Give the children some pictures of pears. The children cut the pears in half and write a homophone on each half of the pear. They can use the pears as puzzles or turn them over and play Memory Game with them.

Tenses

The children read a short text in the present tense. They then re-write the text in the past tense. They compare the two with a partner to determine what makes one text the present tense and one the past tense. This exercise can be done with the future tense as well.

Suffix Unwrapping

Create a list of words with common suffixes at the end of the words. The child then writes the root word and the suffix for each word. This can also be done as a whole class with children writing on whiteboards.

Suffix Unwrapping

smiling		
raked		
bakes		
cooking		
painting		
peeled		
sweeps		
vacuumed		
mixed		
eating		

Suffixes,1-1-1 rule

Teach children the 1-1-1 rule for adding suffixes to root words.

1 Syllable word
1 Final consonant
1 Short middle vowel
Then double the final consonant before adding a suffix beginning with a vowel.
bat-batted
sit-sitting

Prefix Unwrapping

Create a list of words with common prefixes at the beginning. The child then writes the root word and the prefix for each word; this can also be done as a whole class with children writing on whiteboards.

Prefix Unwrapping

unhappy		
impossible		
overcook		
unable		
autobiography		
demotivate		
disagree		
download		
undo		
improve		

Spelling Dictionary

There are lots of excellent spelling dictionaries available. It is impossible to know all the spelling rules in English, so it is always a good idea to look up the rules when teaching a new sound.

Dictation

At first, dictation can be letters on a whiteboard; later, you can extend the children words and then sentences. Dictate sentences and words from the word lists and sentence banks at the back of the book or make up your own.

The children say the sounds, count the sounds and write the word. If the children are writing sentences, then you say the sentences first, the second time they say the sentence with you, and then the third time they count the words in the sentences. Lastly, they write the sentence. Model writing the words or sentences on the board, and the children can self-mark.

Marking spelling

When marking spelling in their written work, do not correct every incorrect word. Pick three or four words that the child should be capable of spelling, underline the part of the word that is wrong, and the child then corrects and re-writes the word.

Child's writes **sn<u>ai</u>k.**
You underline the incorrect part of the word **sn<u>ai</u>k.**
The child self-corrects and writes **snake.**
If the child fails to make the correct spelling, then you can have a conversation with the child to guide them to the correct spelling.

Helpful Spelling Rules

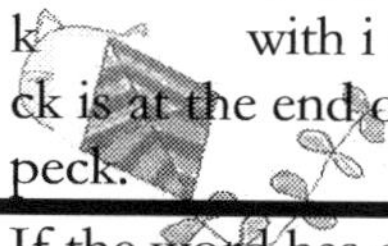

c, k or ck	c with a, u, and o: cat, cut, cod. k with i and e: kite, kelp. ck is at the end of a word or syllable after a short vowel sound: back, peck.
FLoSZ rule	If the word has one vowel and ends in an f, l, s, or z sound, then double the letter: bell, sniff, boss.
j, g or dge	j at the start of a word: jet. g followed by e, i or y: gentle, gym, giant. dge after a short vowel sound at the end of a word: bridge.
x	Usually found at the end of a word: box.
y Cry Baby Rule y saying igh/ ee y saying i	y (Consonant sound) at the start of a word: yes. y says igh at the end of a short word: cry. y says ee at the end of a two-syllable word: baby, happy. y says i when followed by one or two consonants: gym, pyramid.
z or zz	z at the start of a word: zip, zebra. zz at the end of a word with one short vowel sound: fizz.
qu	The queen q always has an umbrella u: quiz.
ch, t or tch	ch is usually at the start of a word: chip. t is before ure or ion: nature, mixture. tch is after a single vowel letter: catch, patch.
th (the) th (moth)	th followed by e usually makes the sound voiced: these. th is unvoiced: moth, cloth.
ai, ee, oa, ey, ea, ie, ou, oe or ue	When two vowels go walking, the first one does the talking. When two vowels are together, say the long sound for the first vowel: aim, feet, boat, key, bead, shoulder, toe, blue.
ow or ou	ow at the end of a syllable: clown, frown. ou at the beginning or middle of a syllable: house, shout.
oi or oy	When the oi sound is inside the word or syllable: join. oy goes at the end of a word: boy, toy.
ai or ay	ai in the middle of words: brain, main. ay is used at the end of a word: play, say.
a-e, e-e, i-e, o-e, or u-e	The e on the end of a split digraph makes the vowel say its name: fade, these, time, note, cube.
a as a schwa sound	When used in an unstressed syllable, the a makes a schwa sound, normally at the end of a word: pizza.
a saying o	After a w or a qu an o sound is written with the letter a: swan, squad.
ue or ew	ew is at the end of a word: new, few.
or, au or ore	or in the beginning, middle or end of a word: for, nor. au is never at the end of a word: sauce, haunt.

	ore in the middle or end of a word: snore, wore.
le, al or el	le is the most common and is found at the end of a word; it adds a syllable to the word: wiggle, title. al is the subsequent most common spelling: metal. el after m, n, r, v, w (mnemonic: most nuns run very well): camel, travel.
m or mb	m is the most common spelling for this sound: mole. mb words are Roman in origin and come at the end of a word: climb, thumb.
kn, gn or n	n is the most common spelling for this sound: net, not. kn are words with Viking origins and are found at the beginning of words: know, knife. gn is usually at the front of a word: gnome.
r or wr	r is the most common spelling choice: rat, rabbit. wr at the beginning of a word: write, wrap.
wh or w	w is the most common spelling for this sound: went, was. wh at the start of a word: wheel, where.
v or ve	v at the beginning of the word: voice, vent. An e must follow a v sound at the end of a word: love, have.
sh, ch, ci, ti or s	sh is the most common spelling: ship, shave. Use ch for words with a French origin. chef, chalet. ci for words that end with cial, cian, or cious: facial, musician, precious. ti for words that end in tion, tious, or tial: caption, nutritious, partial. s for words that end with sion or ssion: decision, mission.
s, se, sc, c or st	A c followed by e, i or y makes an s sound: receipt, ceiling. st is usually in the middle of a word: listen, whistle.
se saying z	se makes a z sound at the end of a word: noise, tease.
Contractions	When two words are joined to create the contracted form, use an apostrophe to replace the missing letters: can't, I'll.
ie saying ee ie saying ai	Place the i before e except after c when the sound is long: ceiling, receipt.
ed	ed makes three different sounds it makes the ed, d or t sound: hunted, robbed, jumped.
Plural Rules s, es or ies	Most times, add an s: dogs, goats. If the word ends in s, ss, x, ch, or sh, add es: boxes, riches. If the plural creates another syllable, then add es as the suffix. When the singular noun ends in an f, change to v, and add es: wolves. When the singular ends in y, drop the y and add ies: babies, berries.
Syllable rules	There is one vowel per syllable: boat, ship. Split after x or ck: box/es, nick/el. Split between compound words: bird/house, light/house. Split VC/CV patterns: sis/ter, af/ter.

	Prefixes and suffixes are syllables: un/do, care/less. Before consonant, le: pur/ple, can/dle.
Prefixes	dis, un, mis, im, in means not: dishonest, unbuckled, misplaced, improper, inactive. re means do again: refill. bi means two: bicycle. tri means three: tricycle. pro means for: proclaim. sub means under or below: subway, submarine de means from: dependant. ex means out of or from: expert. pre means before: prepare.
Suffixes	ment changes adjective to noun: enjoyment. ly means do something: happily. er means more or someone who does something: teacher. ness means being: sickness. est means most: prettiest. ful means full of: wonderful. less means without: careless.
Suffixes 1-1-1 Rule	ed, er one syllable words, one final consonant, one short middle vowel double the final consonant before adding a suffix starting with a vowel: hummed, bigger.
ing	Most verbs add ing: eating, starting. Verbs ending in y, add ing: playing, trying. Verbs ending in e, drop the e and add ing: hoping, riding. Verbs ending in one vowel and one consonant, use the 1-1-1 Rule: and add ing: sitting, jogging. Verbs ending in ie, change ie to y and add ing: dying.
Word Families	at, an, am, ap, ad, ag, ab, ank, ail, ate, ake, and, all, ash ig, ick, ill, id, in, ip, it, ing, ell, ish, ight, ice, ink et, ell, en, ed op, og, ob, ot, ook, ock, ong, one ub, ug, um, un, ut, uck, ump

Tricky Words and Common Exception Words

Use the activities in this chapter to teach spelling words, Tricky Words (Common Exception Words) and High-Frequency Words. Explicitly teach Tricky Words as they often do not come in sound or word families.

We can compare learning to spell a word to a spider web. If the spider tries to hang its web on one line, the web will be destroyed or blown away. However, if it anchors its web on many strings, the web will be strong and last longer. The same goes for learning to spell; if a child only does one thing to learn a new word, like write it down, they will lose the word quickly. However, if they do a few different activities, their brains make lots of connections and retain the knowledge.

Tricky Train

Children need to build meaning and association around words to remember them. Make or download Tricky Train worksheets and laminate them so that they can be reused. Once the children have been taught how to use the chart, they can work through words at their own pace.

1. Write the word in the speech bubble for the child or have them copy the word into the speech bubble. The child says the word; if they cannot read the word, then tell them what the word is, and the child then repeats it.
2. The child counts the sounds and colours in the sound clouds.
3. The child makes the word using letter manipulatives and places them over the sound cloud buttons.
4. The child writes the sounds into the train carts, one sound per cart.
5. The child draws the irregular sound on the train track as a rock.
6. Go through the elements on the train ticket: the child identifies and says the first, middle and last sound. They say any words that rhyme with the word, they count and clap the syllables and identify any blends.
7. The child draws a picture representing the word into the magnifying glass. Help the child to make meaning out of abstract words and draw them. For example, for the word **when**, the child can draw a picture of **when** they are happy.
8. The child writes the word on the line using dots and dashes to underscore the graphs, digraphs and trigraphs. They then spell the word out loud using the letter names, they say any digraphs and trigraphs quicker to develop a rhythm.

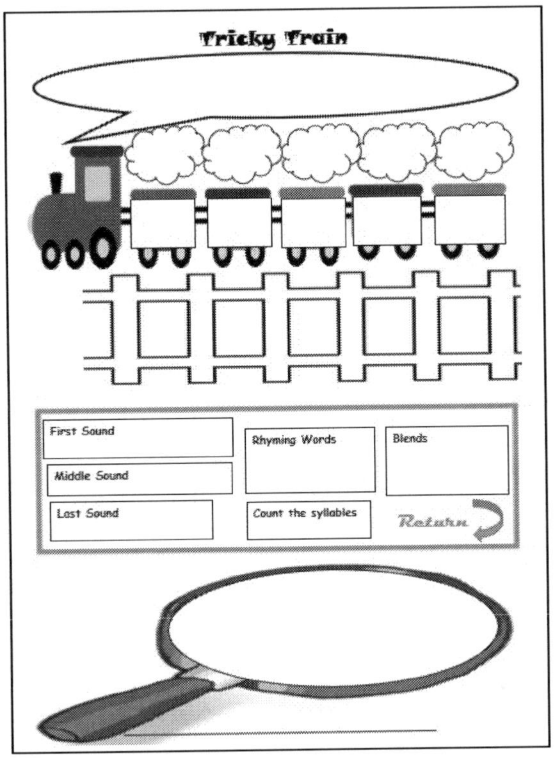

Mnemonics

Mnemonics are memory tricks used to aid the learning and retrieval of information. Teach children to use mnemonics to spell some Tricky Words; the children can also make up their own mnemonics to help them with words they find challenging.

Reception	
but	butterflies under tables
come	can't open my eyes
little	ladybirds in tiny tiaras learn English
said	silly ants in dresses
the	two heavy elephants
they	the and y
was	worms are slimy
went	we eat no treats
Year One	
again	a goat and insect napping
came	can anyone make eggs
made	mice are dancing eagerly
many	mole ate nutty yoghurt
very	vets enjoy real yoghurt
ould	Cally is married to wally, and they have a baby girl called shelly. They are a happy, lucky, ducky family. draw all three ducks on the whiteboard, and then repeat the mnemonic for each one:
could	 oh you lucky ducky
would	 oh you lucky ducky
should	 oh you lucky ducky
Year Two	
because	big elephants can always understand small elephants
Christmas	break the word into christ and mas
every	every vampire eats red yoghurt
eyes	draw eyes onto the word eye
eyes	
father	break the word into fat and her
friend	fri the end of your friend
hear	you hear with your ear
what	what a hat

Word Walls

Create a display in the classroom using the Tricky Words. Refer to the wall when children need to spell a word and have the children read the words and spell them often throughout the week.

Flashcards

Use handheld or PowerPoint flashcards of Tricky Words. The children should read the words automatically and not try to sound them out. They should also spell the words out loud using the letter names.

Tricky Word Pebbles

Write Tricky Words on pebbles or buy ready etched Tricky Word Pebbles. These can then be left on the playground for the children to find, or they can have a word treasure hunt to find them. They can also be kept in the classroom for the children to use during free play. Play a game with the words by placing them upside down on the table. Each child takes turns to turn over a pebble and read it to the group. For anxious children, leave the stones face-up and let them choose which words to read out loud.

Tricky Word Sticks

Write the Tricky Words on lollipop sticks and place them in a jar or tin. The tin can be a working tin, and new words can be added as they are learnt. Here are a few ideas of activities with these words:

The child picks five sticks out of the can, arranges them alphabetically, and then writes down the words.

They pick six sticks, arrange them into the shape of a house, and then write the words.

They pick four sticks and write each word four times.

They could pick a stick and write a sentence using the word.

They pick a few sticks and then read them to a friend or spell each word.

Count It

Use phoneme strips for this activity. Say a word, the child sounds it out and uses counters, Lego, or playdoh balls to represent the sounds in each phoneme box. They then move each manipulative out of the box as they write in their grapheme choice. Lastly, they check the word.

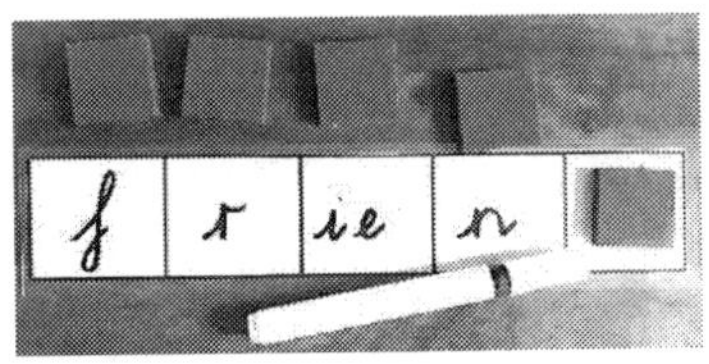

Buttoned Up

Print the Tricky Words on A4 paper. The children then cover the word with buttons, gems, or pebbles.

Pirate Treasure

Write or type Tricky Words onto coins then hide the coins in the sand tray for children to find. The children search for the coins and make a list (by writing all the words down) of their bounty.

Minute to Win It

Use handheld flashcards for this activity and quickly flicks through a set of Tricky Word. The child reads as many words as possible in a minute.

Hidden Word Pictures

Write the letters for a word onto a picture. The child finds all the letters in the image and rearranges them to spell the word.

Tricky Word Stomp

Print out Tricky Words on blue A4 card, cut them into the shape of puddles, and place them on the playground. Then you say a tricky word, and the child finds and stomps on the Tricky Word puddle. Give the child an umbrella and a pair of wellies to make this activity more enjoyable.

Tricky Word Snap

Create a set of Tricky Word cards with matching pairs. Children then share out the cards and play Tricky Word Snap.

Tricky Word Bingo

Make or download some bingo boards with Tricky Words. Each child gets a bingo board, place the word cards in a stack. The children pass the stack around, so each child has the chance to be a caller and read the Tricky Words. The first child to cover their board is the winner.

Tricky Words Memory Game

Print pairs of Tricky Words on cardboard. The children place all the Tricky Words upside down on the table and take turns to turn over two cards; if they get a pair, they can keep it. If they do not get a pair, they turn them back over and the next child has a turn.

Tricky Word Dash

Give each child three or four of the same Tricky Words. They cut their words between the phonemes and place all the muddled-up graphemes in front of them. Then you call out one of the Tricky Words, and they build the word as fast as possible using their puzzle pieces.

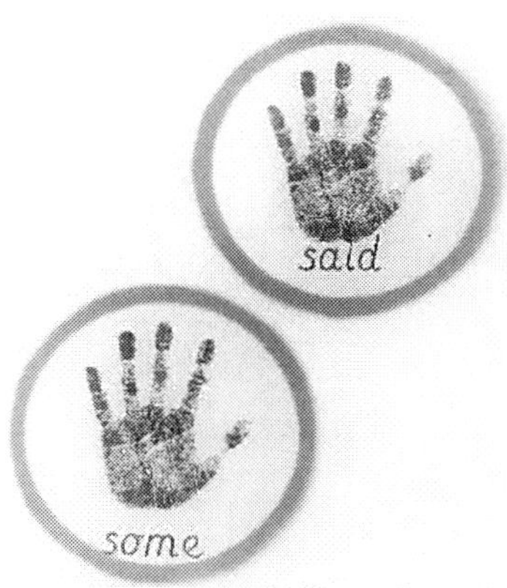

Tricky Word High Five

Print the Tricky Words for the week on handprints. As each child leaves the classroom, they high five the posters and say the words.

Beat the Teacher

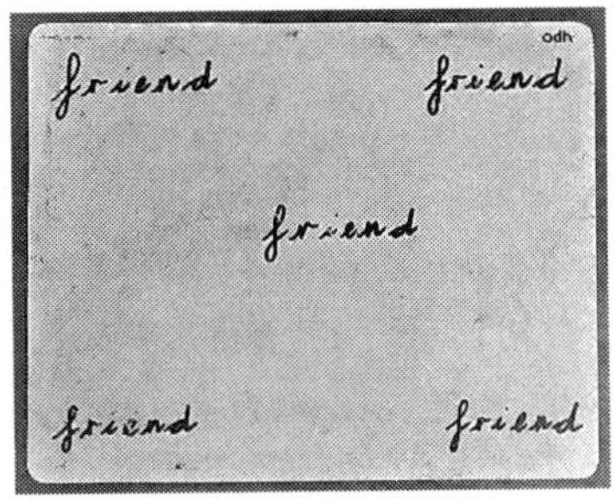

Beat the teacher is a great whole class or group game. Tell the children the Tricky Word and ensure they know how to spell the word. The children then race you to see who can write the word the fastest on each corner and in the centre of their whiteboards. This is a fun game that includes lots of repetition.

Tricky Word Snack

Write the Tricky Words on the fruit snack. The child reads the Tricky Word when they take their snack. Only write on the outside of fruit where the peel is not eaten like bananas and oranges.

Tricky Word Splat

Print the Tricky Words on pictures of flies or bugs. Say a tricky word, and the children use a fly swat to splat the word. To play this game independent of the teacher, make a set of Tricky Word cards, the cards get passed around the group and each child has a turn to be a caller and read the word while the others splat the bugs.

Mini Chalkboards

Mini Chalkboards are great for writing words. Say the word or give the child a word card. The child then sounds out the word and counts the sounds. They take out the required number of chalkboards, write the sounds on the chalkboards and then place them in order. If there is a tricky bit in the word, the child can write this in another colour chalk. There should be one chalkboard per phoneme and not per letter. The child then arranges the word in order and checks that they have spelt the word correctly.

Tricky word Treasure Hunt

Print a set of Tricky Words and hide them around the classroom or playground. The children then go on a treasure hunt to find the Tricky Words. They get one point for finding a word and a bonus point for spelling the word correctly.

Songs

Learn Tricky Words using songs or rhymes. These can be made up, or you can find Tricky Word songs on YouTube. Try to put actions to your Tricky Word songs or rhymes, as this will help children remember them.

Tricky Word Beach Ball

Write Tricky Words on a beach ball. Throw the ball to a child. That child picks a word and reads it, and all the other children write it down on their whiteboards. You can buy ready made Tricky Word balls from Consortium.

Pyramid Writing

Give the child a word. They write the first letter on the first line, then underneath they write the first and second letter, under that, they write the first three letters until the word is complete. They can turn their words into pyramids or sailboats when they are finished.

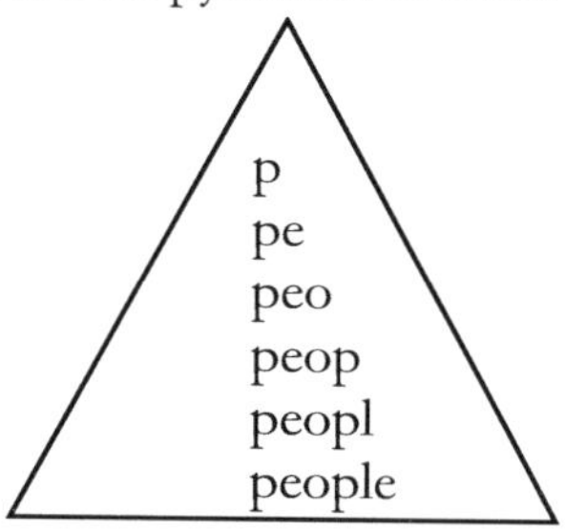

Tricky Word Beach Ball

Write Tricky Words on a beach ball. Throw the ball to a child. That child picks a word and reads it, and all the other children write it down on their whiteboards.

Tricky Word Target Practice

Print out a set of Tricky Words and stick them on the wall. Say a Tricky Word, and the child tries to hit the word with a soft ball. Alternatively, the child can throw the ball and then say which word they have hit.

Bean Bag Toss

Print out some Tricky Words and place them on the floor. Each child then throws a beanbag and says the word. For children with good motor skills, you can say the word, and the child aims for the word.

Worksheet Ideas

Make and print a set of worksheets to keep in your classroom as an emergency spelling activity. Worksheets are as enjoyable to children as other learning activities if used minimally. However, if worksheets are used too often, they lose their impact and worksheet overload results.

Over the Rainbow

Give the children a list of seven words. They write the Tricky Words into the rainbow using the colours of the rainbow. This activity needs to be as colourful as possible as this will help the children remember their words.

Wordsearches

Children with visual difficulties and poor reading skills will find these problematic. Start with small word searches with a few words and give children strategies to solve them. For example, tell the child they have a magic finger that needs to look for the word's first letter. When they find that letter, they look around the letter to see if it makes the word before moving on. Children should be encouraged to look at a word search from left to right and top to bottom like they would if they read a text.

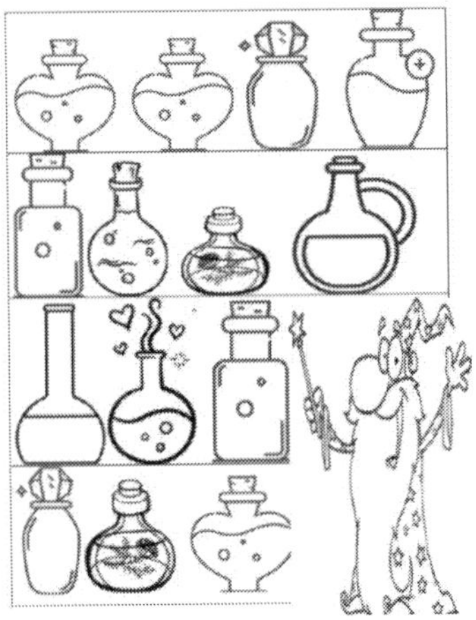

Magic Potion Bottles

The children can write Tricky Words on Sticker labels and use them to label bottles. Then they write sentences using the words and place them inside the bottles. Alternatively, children can label potion bottles on a worksheet and decorate them using lots of colours. The more creative and colourful the activity, the more engaged the students will be and the more they will retain the knowledge.

Crossword Puzzle

Teach children how to complete crossword puzzles; these are good for reinforcing the definitions of new vocabulary and learning the spelling. Create spelling-word crosswords on the website *PuzzleMaker.*

Tricky Word Graffiti Wall

Give each child a cardboard rectangle in different colours. They write a Tricky Word on their cardboard brick and decorate it. Put the bricks together to form a Tricky Word display wall. Alternatively, give each child a worksheet with a wall drawn on it, and they can graffiti their wall using Tricky Words.

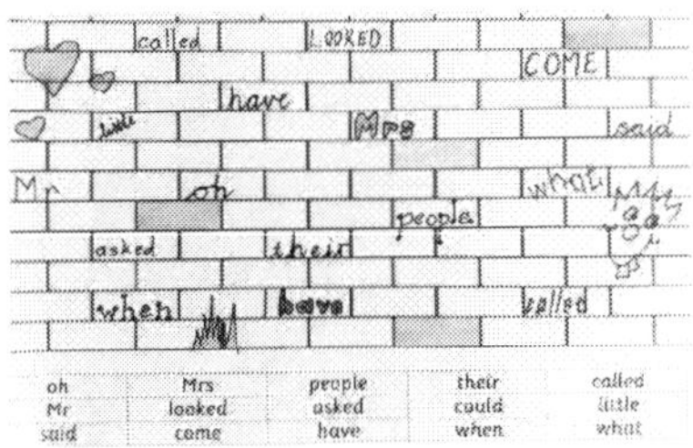

Spiral Spelling

Print a spiral with Tricky Words in a table at the bottom of the page. The child writes the Tricky Words into the spiral turning the page as they go. They then colour and decorate their spiral before cutting it out and hanging it in the classroom. Snakes and ghosts make fun spiral activities.

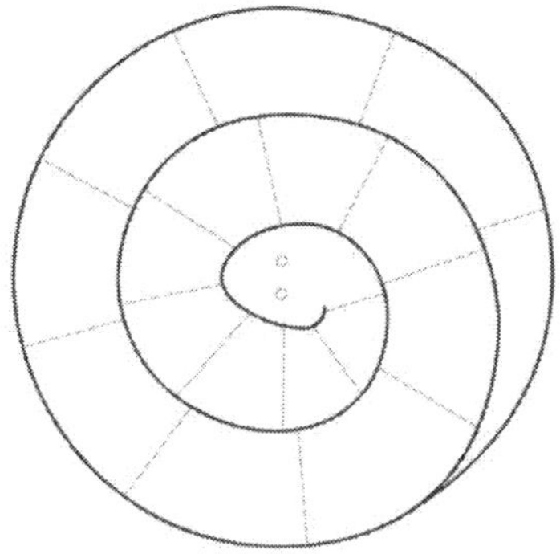

be	you	are	her	was
all	they	my	he	she
we	me	into	to	go

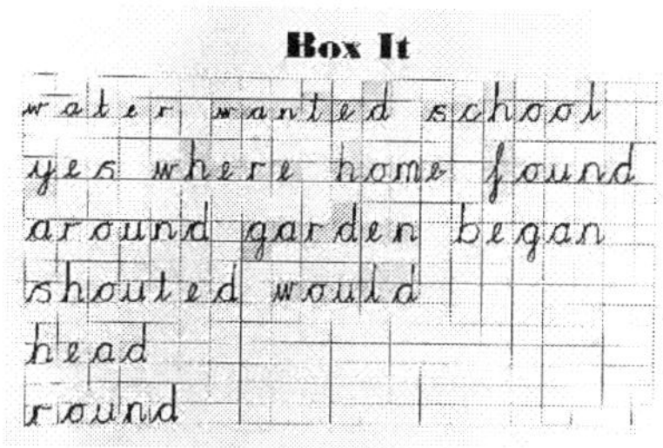

Box It Spelling

Give the child grid paper. They then write Tricky Words in the grids and draw around the shape of the words. Tall and tail letters will use two boxes to help create the shape of the word. Children with spatial relations difficulties will find this activity challenging.

Roll and Read

This activity is aimed at developing automatic recall. Children can play in pairs or small groups. Each child throws the die and then reads all the words associated with the number on their game board. The children can all have the same game board or boards targeting their specific needs, this allows you to place children in mixed ability groups.

.

Roll and read

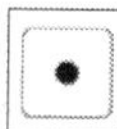	I	no	the	to	go	into
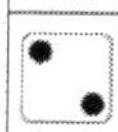	he	she	we	me	be	you
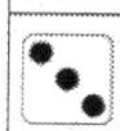	are	her	was	all	they	my
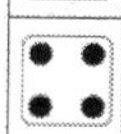	said	have	like	so	do	some
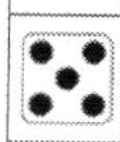	come	little	one	were	there	what
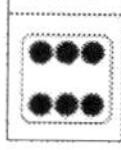	when	out	oh	people	their	called

19 USEFUL RESOURCES

Letters and Sounds

The *Letters and Sounds: Principles and Practice of High-Quality Phonics* book lays out how to teach reading and spelling in a clear, easy to understand step-by-step format. However, it is not a government-endorsed book. The latest guidance by the Department for Education states that the Letters and Sounds book was only ever meant to be a handbook, and schools were expected to build their own phonics programme (2021). For schools who want to improve their practice, the government guidance is that: "Letters and Sounds is not fit for purpose and does not provide the support, guidance, resources or training needed" (2021).

Smart Kids

Smart Kids makes great games and resources for teaching phonics. All their activities are arranged into phases and are colour coded. It is also the only place I have found that sells the *Letters and Sounds Teacher's Manuel.*

THRASS

My first introduction to Phonics was through a programme called THRASS. THRASS is an acronym for Teaching Handwriting Reading and Spelling Skills and was developed by educational psychologist Alan Davies. It has a wealth of resources, stories, software, and tools. I can honestly say that my spelling improved when I learnt how to use and teach using the THRASS system. The training available with THRASS is far superior to any other phonics training I have completed. This system is hugely popular in Australia, South Africa, and Botswana but has not had the same level of popularity in the UK. If you are looking for a programme for your school, it is worth considering the THRASS system.

Jolly Phonics

I first became aware of the scientific basis for the use of *Jolly Phonics* when I read Dianne McGuinness book *Early Reading Instruction; What Science Really Tells us about how to teach reading*. She goes through all the most popular methods for the teaching of reading over the last century and states that the programme with the best scientifically proven results is *Jolly Phonics.* I quickly did the *Jolly Phonics* online course and have been a huge fan ever since.

Jolly Phonics is a multi-sensory, active (programme), specifically designed for young children (Lloyd, 2010). The computer software is easy to use, and the children love the stories, songs, and games. The books are old fashioned and could do with a revamp, but the content is excellent, and they have a wide variety of resources. I would recommend *The Phonics Handbook* by Sue Lloyd and Phonics Teacher's Book. They also have an excellent online CPD course that is relatively inexpensive but highly informative.

LCP Phonics

This system is great for new teachers as it lays out the long term, medium term and short-term plans and has every lesson planned for you saving on planning time. You can pick up the guide and teach the lesson. The progression of lessons is well-paced and logical, and you know that everything has been taught. However, I found the programme a little dry, so you will need to be creative to keep the children interested.

Alphablocks

Alphablocks is brilliant. Children love these short little films in which "blocks" join to make words. I find children start blending words quickly when exposed to Alphablocks as it clearly models blending. You can buy these in DVD sets that are progressive and develop their reading from single sounds to more complex digraphs, trigraphs and split digraphs. The books can be used in conjunction with the DVDs. If you use the books, then I suggest you watch an episode of Alphablocks to understand better how they want the child to read the book. I tried the books before the DVD's and hated them; only once I watched the videos did, I understand how they wanted the child to sound out the words. I am probably the only one who made that silly mistake, but once I understood, the series and books became a gold mine to me!

Phonics Play

Phonics Play is a subscription website, and I would suggest you try to get your school to sign up for the monthly fee. They have lovely flashcards and games that the children enjoy. The games are divided into phases, and I have found them invaluable leading up to the phonics assessment when you are trying to cram in as much revision as possible.

The Oxford Reading Tree

The Oxford Reading Scheme is lovely. They have modern stories and pictures that appeal to young children. They are arranged progressively, so the books are never too hard or easy for the child and are now also available in electronic versions—no more worn old books, sticky from someone's spilt yoghurt. Electronic books are great because they last longer, are easy to access, and have a massive library of titles available and are good for the environment. Most schools are opting for a combination of both electronic and print books.

Bug Club Books

Bug club books are short phonics-based books that the children enjoy. They have the sounds and words printed on the back cover and some teaching ideas on the front cover. This makes them particularly useful for small group intervention groups and guided reading activities.

PhonicBooks

PhonicBooks are written for beginner and catch-up readers. According to their website, they are arranged into a "highly-structured phonics sequence." The text is Dyslexia friendly and printed on cream pages. The illustrations are modern and colourful, High-Frequency words are "introduced slowly," and each book has a game to consolidate new knowledge and a vocabulary page. They also have a wealth of free resources for teachers on their website, including phonics information videos and reading diagnostic assessment tools. Talisman cards are also available through PhonicBooks.

Twinkl

Twinkl has anything you could want for your classroom, activities, planning, intervention, displays and presentations. They are a subscription website but are well worth the cost; they are amazing!

Write Dance

Write Dance is a programme specifically developed to use music and play to develop young children's fine motor skills. It can be done with the whole class or with smaller groups.

Sing-Along Handwriting

Sing-Along Handwriting is a great app to support the teaching and learning of handwriting. It is simple, easy to use and cheap. Each letter is taught with a rhyme that is easy to remember. I recommend this app to parents as children can be left with the app, and they will learn to write without any expert instruction from the teacher or parent.

Mighty Writer

Mighty Writer is a learning resource for classrooms. It is excellent for teaching writing and sentence structure. They provide the equipment as well as training and have good follow up services.

Brain Gym

Brain Gym is a programme of short physical activities that develop the skills needed for the body to work and learn optimally. They recall the movements natural in the child's first few years of life. The teacher can use a book to do brain gym exercises, complete a course or become a facilitator. More information is available on the edu-k website.

Consortium

Consortium is a stationery supplier for schools. They have an excellent range of good quality, safe and affordable tools, toys, and stationery. In addition, they have lots of ready-made phonics games and resources that make planning more manageable and less time-consuming. Rotate the resources between classes, so children always have new and exciting things to use for their learning.

Amazon

Amazon has a wide range of educational toys and activities. They also have unique resources like Montessori equipment that cannot be found in local shops or stationery suppliers.

MyCuteGraphics

MyCuteGraphics is a website with gorgeous royalty-free child-friendly images in both colour and black and white. Use them to create worksheets, presentations or displays.

PuzzleMaker

PuzzleMaker. Discovery Education is a website where you can create your own word puzzles. You can make word searches, crosswords, or more complicated puzzles. It also allows you to choose the case but not the font.

20 SOUND LISTS

Phase Two Sounds

s	socks	a	apple	t	tap	p	pot
i	ink	n	nose	m	mouse	d	dog
g	goat	o	orange	c	cat	k	king
ck	duck	e	egg	u	umbrella	r	rat
h	hat	b	bat	f	fish	ff	muffin
l	leaf	ll	jelly	ss	hiss		

Phase Three Sounds

j	jelly	v	vet	w	wind	x	fox
y	yellow	z	zebra	zz	fizz	qu	queen
ch	chip	sh	ship	th	thumb	th	then
ng	king	ai	rain	ee	leek	igh	light
oa	goat	oo	moon	oo	book	ar	car
or	fork	ur	fur	ow	cow	oi	coin
ear	beard	air	chair	ure	cure	er	fern

Phase Four Blends

st	stone	nd	hand	mp	lamp	nt	tent
nk	ink	ft	gift	sk	skunk	lt	belts
lp	help	lf	elf	lk	milk	pt	script
xt	text	tr	tree	dr	drink	gr	green
cr	crab	br	brown	fr	frog	bl	blue
fl	flag	gl	glue	pl	plug	cl	claw
sl	sleep	sp	spoon	st	stop	tw	twig
sm	smell	pr	printer	sc	scarf	sk	skunk
sn	snail	nch	lunch	scr	scream	shr	shrimp
thr	three	str	string				

Phase Five Vowel Sound Families		Short Vowel Sounds				
	a ant					
	e egg	ea bread				
	i ink	y pyramid	e rocket	ui guitar		
	o octopus	(w)a wasp	ho honest			
	u umbrella	o won				
	oo book	u bull				
Long Vowel Sounds						
	ai rain	ay play	ey grey	a-e cake	ea great	a baby
	ee bee	y pony ie genie	ey key (c)ei ceiling	ea bead	e me	e-e these
	igh light	i-e pine	y sky	i lion	ie pie	
	oa goat	oe toe	o no	ow snow	o-e bone	ou shoulder
	u-e cube	u uniform	ew dew	ue argue		
	oo moon	ew chew	u-e prune	ue blue	ui fruit	ou soup
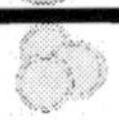	oi coin	oy boy	uoy buoy			
	ow cow	ou house	ough drought			
	er ladder	ar collar	or doctor	a pizza		
Controlled R Vowels						
	air chair	are mare	ear pear	ere where	aer aeroplane	
	ar car	al calf	a bath			
	ir bird	ur fur	ear pearl	er stern	or worm	our journey
	or fork	aw paw ore more	our pour augh caught	oor door ar war	al walk ough bought	au haunted
	ear beard	eer deer	ere sphere	ier pier		ure cure

Phase Five Consonant Sound Families	Consonant Sounds					
	b bat	bb rabbit				
	c cat	ck sock	k king	ch school	qu croquet	cc soccer
	d dog	dd middle	ed filled			
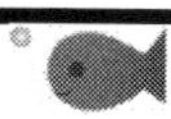	f fish	ff waffle	ph dolphin	gh laugh		
	g grapes	gg egg	gh ghost	gu guest	gue catalogue	
	h hat	wh whole				
	j jelly	g giraffe	dge bridge	ge cage	di soldier	gy gym
	l leg	ll hill	le apple	el camel		
	m mouse	mb lamb	mm hammer	mn autumn		
	n nest	nn bunny	kn knight	gn gnome	pn pneumonia	
	ng king	n(k) ink	ngue tongue			
	p pig	pp hippo				
	qu queen				x box	
	r rainbow	rr barrel	wr wrist	rh rhyme		
	s sun	ss kiss	c city	se horse	st listen	sc scissors
	t tap	tt mitten	ed jumped			
	v vet	ve give	f of			
	w wig	wh whale	u queen			
	y yo-yo	i opinion	j hallelujah			
	z zebra	zz buzz	ze maze	se rose	s bends	ss scissors
	ch chips	tch watch	t picture			
	sh shell	ch chef	s sugar	ti station	si session	ci social
	s treasure	si division		th tooth		th feather

21 WORD LISTS

Tricky Words
Phase Two

I	no	the	to	go	into

Phase Three

he	she	we	me	be	you
are	her	was	all	they	my

Phase Four

said	have	like	so	do	some
come	little	one	were	there	what
when	out				

Phase Five

oh	Mrs	people	their	called	Mr
looked	asked	could			

High Frequency Words

Phase Two

a	an	as	at	if
in	is	it	of	off
on	can	dad	had	back
and	get	big	him	his
not	got	up	mum	but
put	the	to	I	no
go	into			

Phase Three

will	that	this	then	them
with	see	for	now	down
look	too	he	she	we
me	be	was	you	they
all	are	my	her	

Phase Four

went	it's	from	children	just
help	said	have	like	so
do	some	come	were	there
little	one	when	out	what

Phase Five

don't	old	I'm	by	time
house	about	your	day	made
came	make	here	saw	very
oh	their	people	Mr	Mrs
looked	called	asked	could	

The Following One Hundred High Frequency Words

water	didn't	yes	through	lots	small
away	ran	play	way	need	car
good	know	take	been	that's	couldn't
want	bear	thought	stop	baby	three
over	can't	dog	must	fish	head
how	again	well	red	gave	king
did	cat	find	door	mouse	town
man	long	more	right	something	I've
going	things	I'll	sea	bed	around
where	new	round	these	may	every
would	after	tree	began	still	garden
or	wanted	magic	boy	found	fast
took	eat	shouted	animals	live	only
school	everyone	us	never	say	many
think	our	other	next	soon	laughed
home	two	food	first	night	
who	has	fox	work	narrator	

The Last 100 High Frequency Words

let's	clothes	different	friends	wind	white
much	tell	let	box	wish	coming
suddenly	key	girl	dark	eggs	he's
told	fun	which	grandad	once	river
another	place	inside	there's	please	liked
great	mother	run	looking	thing	giant
why	sat	any	end	stopped	looks
cried	boat	under	than	ever	use
keep	window	hat	best	miss	along
room	sleep	snow	better	most	plants
last	feet	air	hot	cold	dragon
jumped	morning	trees	sun	park	pulled
because	queen	bad	across	lived	we're
even	each	tea	gone	birds	fly
am	book	top	hard	duck	grow
before	its	eyes	floppy	horse	
gran	green	fell	really	rabbit	

Common Exception Words
Year One Words

the	a	do	to	today	me
of	said	says	are	were	she
was	is	his	has	I	we
you	your	they	be	he	no
go					

Year Two Words

door	floor	poor	because	find	kind
mind	behind	child	children	wild	climb
most	only	both	old	cold	gold
hold	told	every	great	break	steak
pretty	beautiful	after	fast	last	past
father	class	grass	pass	plant	path
bath	hour	move	prove	improve	sure
sugar	eye	could	should	would	who
whole	any	many	clothes	busy	people
water	again	half	money	Mr	Mrs
parents	Christmas	everybody	even		

Combined Words Lists

The following words lists have been organised by Year Group. The Reception list is comprised of the Phase Two, Three and Four Tricky Words and High Frequency Words. The Year One list is the Phase Five Tricky Words, the Year One Common Exception Words and the first 100 High Frequency Words. The Year Two List comprises of the Year Two Common Exception Words and the next 100 High Frequency Words.

Reception Combined Word List

a	all	an	and	are	as
at	back	be	big	but	can
children	come	dad	do	down	for
from	get	go	got	had	have
he	help	her	him	his	I
if	in	into	is	it	it's
just	like	little	look	me	mum
my	no	not	now	of	off
on	one	out	put	said	see
she	so	some	that	the	there
them	then	they	this	to	too
up	was	we	went	were	when
will	with	you			

Year One Combined Word List

about	again	after	animals	around	asked
away	baby	bed	bear	began	been
boy	by	called	cat	came	can't
car	could	couldn't	day	did	didn't
dog	door	don't	eat	every	everyone
fast	find	first	fish	food	found
fox	garden	gave	going	good	has
head	here	home	house	how	I'll
I'm	I've	king	looked	laughed	live
long	lots	made	make	many	man
may	magic	mouse	more	Mr	Mrs
must	narrator	need	new	never	next
night	oh	old	only	or	other
our	over	people	play	ran	right
round	say	says	saw	red	sea
shouted	small	something	soon	still	stop
take	today	took	that's	these	three
thought	through	their	things	think	time
town	tree	two	us	very	want
wanted	water	way	well	where	who
work	would	yes	your		

Year Two Combined Word List

across	am	air	along	another	any
bad	bath	beautiful	because	before	best
better	birds	boat	book	both	box
break	busy	child	Christmas	class	climb
clothes	cold	coming	cried	dark	different
dragon	duck	each	eggs	end	even
ever	every	everybody	eye	eyes	fast
father	feet	fell	find	floor	floppy
fly	friends	fun	girl	giant	gold
gone	gran	grandad	grass	great	green
grow	hard	half	hat	he's	hold
horse	hot	hour	improve	inside	it's
jumped	keep	key	kind	last	let
let's	lived	liked	looking	looks	many
mind	miss	money	morning	most	mother
move	much	old	once	only	parents
park	pass	past	path	place	plant
plants	please	poor	pretty	prove	pulled
queen	rabbit	really	river	room	run
sat	should	sleep	snow	steak	stopped
suddenly	sugar	sun	sure	tea	tell
under	use	than	there's	told	top
trees	water	we're	white	who	whole
why	wild	window	wind	wish	

22 PHONEME WORD LISTS

Phase Two Phoneme Word List

s a t	**i**	**p**	**n**	**c**	**k**
a	it	pat	ant	can	kid
at	sit	pip	an	cans	kin
sat		pit	nip	cap	kip
		sap	pan	caps	kit
		sip	pin	cat	tank
		sips	snap	cats	
		tap	snip	cod	
		taps	spin	cop	
		tip	tan	cops	
		tips	tin	cot	
		Unvoiced		If the following vowel is **a, o,** or **u.**	If the next vowel is an **i** or an **e,** use **k.**
ck	**e**	**h**	**r**	**m**	**d**
kick	neck	hack	crack	camp	and
pack	net	hat	crisp	him	dad
duck	peck	hats	ran	man	den
pick	pen	hectic	rap	map	did
sack	pest	hen	rat	mat	had
sick	pet	hens	rest	met	hid
snack	set	hint	rip	mill	mad
stack	step	hip	scrap	miss	red
stick	ten	hiss	trap	ram	sad
back	tent	hit	trip	stem	sand
At the end of a word or syllable after a short vowel sound.					

g	**o**	**u**	**l**	**ll**	**f**
gap	dog	cup	clap	bell	fan
gas	drop	mud	lap	doll	fat
get	got	mug	laptop	dull	fig
gran	not	mum	leg	fill	fin
grandad	on	run	let	hill	fit
grin	pond	sun	lid	mill	fog
grip	pot	sunset	lit	sell	frog
peg	rock	truck	lot	smell	from
rag	sock	tuck	plan	spell	fun
tag	stop	up	lost	tell	if
				One vowel and ends in an **l** sound, then use **ll.**	Unvoiced

ff	**b**	**ss**	
bluff	back	boss	
cliff	bad	dress	
cuff	bag	fuss	
fluff	bat	hiss	
gruff	bed	kiss	
huff	bet	less	
muffin	big	mass	
off	bus	mess	
puff	but	moss	
	rabbit	press	
If the word has one vowel and ends in an **f** sound, then use **ff**.		If the word has one vowel and ends in an **s** sound, then use **ss.**	

Phase Three Phoneme Word List

j	**v**	**w**	**x**	**y**	**z**
jab	van	cobweb	box	yak	zap
jacket	vat	swim	exit	yam	zen
jam	vent	twig	fox	yap	zest
jet	vest	wag	mix	yard	zigzag
jig	vet	wax	next	yell	zip
job	vet	web	ox	yelp	zit
jog	vivid	wig	six	yes	
jump		will	tax	yet	
junk		win	taxi	yuck	
just		wind	wax		
At the start of a word.		Common spelling choice.	Usually at the end of a word.	At the start of a word.	At the start of a word

zz	**qu**	**ch**	**sh**	**th**	**th**
buzz	liquid	chap	cash	feather	cloth
fizz	quack	check	dish	slither	moth
jazz	queen	chicken	fish	that	thank
	quest	chill	hush	the	thick
	quick	children	rush	them	thin
	quill	chip	shed	then	think
	quilt	chop	shell	this	thirteen
	quit	much	ship		three
	quiz	rich	wish		tooth
	squid	such	shop		with
The word has one vowel, then use **zz**.	The queen **q** always has an umbrella **u**.	Usually at the start of a word.	Common spelling choice.	**th** followed by **e** usually makes the sound voiced.	Unvoiced

ng	**ai**	**ee**	**igh**	**oa**	**oo**
things	aim	three	fight	boat	boot
hang	bait	tree	high	coat	food
king	hail	feet	light	foam	moon
long	mail	jeep	midnight	goat	roof
ring	pain	keep	might	load	root
along	rain	see	night	loaf	spoon
sing	sail	need	right	moat	too
song	tail	sleep	sight	road	zoo
swing	train	queen	tight	soap	zoom
wing	wait	green	tonight	toad	
	When two vowels are together, say the long sound for the first vowel.	When two vowels are together, say the long sound for the first vowel.		One syllable words. When two vowels are together, say the long sound for the first vowel.	

or	ur	ow	oo	ar	er
born	burn	clown	book	bar	better
cord	burnt	cow	cook	bark	boxer
cork	burp	crown	foot	car	dinner
corn	curl	down	good	card	hammer
for	fur	frown	hood	cartoon	ladder
fork	hurt	how	hook	farm	letter
fort	hurt	now	look	hard	letter
sort	surf	owl	took	hard	rocker
torn	turn	sow	wood	park	summer
worn	turnip	town	wool	shark	supper
		At the end of a syllable.			

air	ure	oi	ear
air	cure	boil	beard
chair	manure	boil	clear
fair	mature	coil	dear
hair	pure	coin	ear
lair	secure	join	fear
pair	sure	oil	gear
stair	lure	point	hear
		soil	near
		spoil	rear
		tinfoil	year
		When the **oi** sound is inside the word or syllable.	

Phase Four Phoneme Word List
Initial Consonant Blends

bl	cl	fl	pl	sl	tw
blab black bland bled bleed blend blog bloom blur	clam clamp clap cling clink clip clod clogs club	flag flap flash flat fleck fleet flesh flint flip	plan plastic plod plop plot plug plum plump plus	slap sled sleep slept slim slip slob slog slot	tweed tweet twig twin twist twit
br	**cr**	**dr**	**fr**	**gr**	**tr**
brag bran brand brat brick bring brisk broth brown brush	crab cram cramp crash crept crisp croc crop cross crust	drag drench dress drift drill drip droop drop drug drum	frantic free fresh frill frisk frog from frost froth frown	grab gran green grim grin grinch grip grog growl grunt	track train tramp trap tree treetop trend trim trip trust
pr	**sn**	**st**	**sc**	**sm**	**sw**
pram preen press prick print promo proof prop props	snack snag snail snap sniff snip snoop snort snuck	stack stamp stand star steel steps stop stud stun	scam scan scar scat scoff scoop sculk scull scalp	smack smart smash smell smith smock smog smooth smug	swam swell swift swig swim swing swoon swoop swot
spr	**str**	**shr**	**thr**	**scr**	**sp**
sprain spring sprint	strain strap string strip stroll strop strum strut	shrank shred shrill shrimp shrink shrub shrug	thrash three thrift thrill throb thrush thrust	scrap screen script scroll scrub scruff scruffy scrum	span spark spat sped speech spend spin spit

Final Consonant Blends

lb	ld	lf	lm	lk	sp
bulb	cold	elf	film	bulk	crisp
	fold	golf		hulk	lisp
	held	shelf		milk	wisp
	sold	gulf		sculk	
	old	shelf		silk	
	bold	self		sulk	
	gold	himself			
		bookshelf			
lp	**lt**	**ct**	**ft**	**nt**	**sk**
gulp	belt	duct	drift	ant	desk
help	bolt	fact	gift	bent	disk
kelp	colt	impact	lift	burnt	husk
pulp	felt	infect	loft	dent	risk
welp	holt	inject	shift	hunt	tusk
yelp	melt	insect	soft	sent	
	quilt	pact	swift	joint	
	split	strict	theft	print	
	tilt	tact	tuft	tent	
				went	
pt	**st**	**nch**	**mp**	**nd**	**nk**
crept	best	bench	camp	band	bank
kept	boost	bunch	champ	bend	blink
script	chest	finch	chimpanzee	bond	bunk
slept	frost	French	damp	grand	drank
swept	gust	hunch	hump	hand	drunk
tempt	just	lunch	lamp	land	ink
wept	lost	munch	limp	mend	link
	must	pinch	plump	pond	sank
	nest	punch	ramp	sand	sink
	zest	winch	thump	wind	skunk

Phase Five Phoneme Word List

ay	a	ey	a-e	eigh	ea
Friday	acorn	disobey	base	eight	great
may	angel	grey	cake	eighteen	break
Monday	apricot	obey	came	eighty	steak
play	apron	prey	take	freight	
pray	baby	survey	lake	neighbour	
Saturday	bacon	they	made	neighbourhood	
say	bagel		make	sleigh	
Sunday	basic		place	weight	
way	lady		shake		
away	nation		gave		
day	native				
At the end of a word			The **e** on the end of a split digraph makes the vowel say its name.		

ere	ear	are	a	al
everywhere	bear	bare	branch	balm
nowhere	pear	care	fast	calf
somewhere	swear	dare	faster	calm
there	tear	fare	father	half
where	wear	glare	grass	palm
		hare	last	
		scare	mast	
		share	pass	
		square	password	
		stare	past	
			path	
			ar in the south of England.	

ey	ea	ie	y	e	e-e
chimney	bead	belief	baby	be	complete
donkey	bean	chief	ferry	decent	even
honey	eat	field	funny	frequent	extreme
jockey	each	genie	every	he	gene
key	meat	priest	happy	me	scene
money	please	relief	floppy	recent	theme
monkey	read	shield	penny	she	these
trolley	tea	shriek	silly	we	
turkey	sea	thief	really	began	
valley	steam	yield	very	we're	
When two vowels are together, say the long sound for the first vowel.			At the end of a two-syllable word.		The **e** on the end of a split digraph makes the vowel say its name.

ea	ere	eer	o	a	oy
bread	adhere	beer	something	gorilla	annoy
breakfast	here	career	come	panda	annoying
dead	interfere	cheer	done	pizza	boy
deadly	severe	deer	Monday	banana	destroy
feather	sphere	peer	month	alone	enjoy
head		sheer	mother	ago	joy
heaven		steer	nothing	comma	oyster
instead		veer	other	idea	royal
read			some		toy
ready			another		
				Schwa sound. Normally at the end of a word.	At the end of a word or syllable.

er	or	ear	ir	ou	ough
fern	word	early	bird	about	drought
her	work	earn	birth	around	plough
herbal	world	earnest	first	found	
herbs	worm	earth	girl	house	
jerky	worse	heard	shirt	loudest	
perky	worship	learn	sir	mouse	
permanent	worst	pearl	skirt	our	
servant	worth	rehearsal	thirsty	out	
stern	worthy	search	thirteen	shout	
verb			thirty	round	
				Beginning or middle of a syllable.	

y	**ui**
bicycle	biscuit
crystal	build
cygnet	guitar
Egypt	
gym	
mystery	
pyramid	
pyjamas	

ie	**i-e**	**i**	**y**
cried	inside	behind	by
denied	invite	blind	cry
die	kite	child	dry
dried	wife	find	fly
fried	like	giant	fry
lie	pine	kind	my
pie	ripe	mild	reply
spied	shine	mind	sky
tie	white	remind	spy
tried	time	wild	why
At the end of a word. Or to replace the **y** when the suffix **ed** is added to a root word.	The **e** on the end of a split digraph makes the vowel say its name.		When a short word ends with an **igh** sound.

a	(qu)**a**
swamp	qualify
swan	quantity
wallet	quarry
was	squabble
wash	squadron
wasp	squalid
watch	squander
what	squash
swallow	squat
what	squad

After a **w** or a **qu** an **a** makes an **o** sound

u-e	**u**	**ew**	**ue**
computer	duty	dew	argue
cube	future	few	cue
cute	human	knew	due
fuse	music	nephew	hue
huge	stupid	new	rescue
mule	tuba	news	statue
muse	unicorn	newt	sue
refuge	union	renew	value
tube	unit	stew	venue
use			
The **e** on the end of a split digraph makes the vowel say its name.			

o-e	o	ou	oe	ow	ough
alone	cold	boulder	doe	arrow	dough
bone	don't	mould	dominoes	grow	dough
envelope	go	mouldy	foe	low	nut
explode	gold	shoulder	goes	shadow	though
home	going		heroes	show	
note	told		hoe	slow	
pole	most		potatoes	snow	
stone	no		toe	know	
those	old		tomatoes	swallow	
woke	only		woe	window	
The **e** on the end of a split digraph makes the vowel say its name.		When two vowels are together, we say the long sound for the first vowel.			

ue	ew	u-e	ou	ui	o
blue	blew	brute	group	bruise	do
clue	chew	exclude	soup	cruise	to
cue	crew	flute	troupe	fluid	who
duel	drew	June	you	fruit	into
fuel	flew	plume	through	juice	
glue	grew	prune		nuisance	
issue	grew	rude		ruin	
tissue	screw	rule		suit	
true	threw	salute			
At the end of a word. When two vowels are together, say the long sound for the first vowel.	At the end of a word				

aw	au	our	oor	augh	ore
claw	August	court	door	caught	before
crawl	author	four	doorstep	daughter	chore
draw	automatic	fourth	doorstop	haughty	core
jaw	fraud	mourn	floor	naughty	more
law	haul	pour	poor	taught	score
lawn	haunted	tour	poorly		shore
paw	jaunty	tournament			snore
raw	launch	your			sore
saw	sauce				store
yawn	staunch				wore
In the middle or at the end of a word.	Never at the end of a word.				At the end of a word.

al	ar	ough	ch	tch	t
ball	towards	bought	chemical	catch	adventure
beanstalk	war	fought	chemist	ditch	capture
call	warm	ought	chord	fetch	creature
fall		thought	chorus	kitchen	feature
hall			Christmas	match	future
stalk			chronic	patch	mixture
talk			headache	pitch	nature
walk			school	scratch	picture
wall			technical	stitches	puncture
				witch	signature
	After a **w**.			After a single vowel letter.	When the **ch** sound is before **ure** or **ion.**

ph	wh	dge	g	le	el
alphabet	who	badge	danger	apple	camel
dolphin	whoever	badger	energy	bottle	squirrel
elephant	whole	dodge	gem	cattle	tinsel
graph	whom	fudge	gentle	giggle	towel
nephew	whose	hedge	giant	jumble	travel
phantom		ledge	ginger	little	tunnel
phonics		lodge	giraffe	middle	
prophet		lodger	gymnastics	table	
sphinx		sledge	magic	title	
telephone		wedge	magician	wiggle	
		After a short vowel sound at the end of a word	A **g** followed by the letter **e, i** or **y.**	At the end of a word, Adds a syllable to the word.	After **m, n, r, s, w, v, s**

mb	gn	kn	wr	wh	ve
bomb	assign	knee	winkle	what	above
climb	design	knew	wrap	wheel	behave
comb	gnat	knickers	wreck	when	brave
crumb	gnaw	knife	wren	where	gave
dumb	gnaw	knight	wrestle	which	give
lamb	gnome	knit	write	while	have
limb	gnu	knob	written	whisper	live
numb	resign	knock	wrong	whistle	love
plumbing	sign	know	wrote	white	save
thumb		knuckle	wry	why	wave
At the end of a word	At the beginning of a word.		At the beginning of a word.	At the start of a word.	An e must follow a v sound at the end of a word.

ch	ci	ti	s
brochure	ancient	caption	compression
chalet	artificial	mention	decision
chef	facial	motion	discussion
machine	financial	nutritious	fusion
	glacial	partial	mission
	musician	patience	passion
	official	position	session
	precious	potential	sugar
	social	potion	sure
	special	station	vision
Words with a French origin.	Words that end with **cial, cian**, or **cious.**	Words that end in **tion, tious,** or **tial.**	Words that end with **sion** or **ssion.**

se	sc	c	st	s	se
cease	crescent	acid	bristle	casual	because
crease	descent	advice	castle	leisure	browse
grease	fascinate	bicycle	Christmas	pleasure	cheese
grouse	fascinating	cell	glisten	television	ease
horse	scene	cellar	jostle	treasure	noise
house	scenery	central	listen	usual	pause
loose	scent	city	rustle	vision	please
mouse	science	ice	soften	visit	tease
purse	scissors	ice-cream	whistle		
		icicle	wrestle		
		A c followed by **e**, **i** or **y** makes an **s** sound.	Usually, in the middle of a word.		The **z** sound at the end of a word.

Phase Six Phoneme Word List

ed	**ing**	**ing**	**en**	**ness**	**less**
cried	caring	giving	broaden	coldness	careless
jumped	carrying	having	flatten	darkness	clueless
landed	dancing	living	lengthen	fondness	helpless
liked	eating	loving	loosen	happiness	homeless
listened	feeling	saving	moisten	homelessness	hopeless
looked	flying		shorten	loneliness	painless
shredded	getting		soften	sadness	penniless
smiled	hoping		straighten	sickness	powerless
stopped	hopping		tighten	stillness	restless
wanted	meeting		toughen	tiredness	useless
Change a verb to past tense by adding **ed** if it ends in a consonant after a short vowel, double the consonant.	Present continuous. When you add **ing** to words that end in **ve**, drop the e.		The suffix **en** turns adjectives into verbs.	The suffix **ness** turns an adjective into a noun	The suffix **less** turns a noun or verb into an adjective.

er	**er**	**ier**	**est**	**ment**	**ful**
carer	bigger	angrier	biggest	advertisement	beautiful
listener	fatter	bumpier	coldest	agreement	careful
player	longer	crazier	fastest	amazement	hopeful
reader	nicer	dirtier	funniest	amusement	mouthful
rider	richer	earlier	hottest	development	painful
ruler	taller	foggier	longest	disagreement	playful
runner	thinner	funnier	nicest	employment	powerful
teacher	whiter	hairier	smallest	enjoyment	restful
worker	colder	happier	tallest	entertainment	thoughtful
	hotter	messier	whitest	payment	wonderful
	wetter				restful
Suffix **er** is added to a root word to make it the person who does the task.	A comparative adjective is used to compare two objects, animals, people, or ideas.		Superlatives are used to compare two or more objects, people, animals, or things.	Turn a verb into a noun.	Turn a noun or verb into an adjective, meaning full of/lots of something.

ly	ly	ly	un	y
badly	annually	brotherly	unafraid	bony
carefully	daily	friendly	unclear	cheeky
heavily	fortnightly	homely	undo	funny
kindly	hourly	motherly	unemployed	hairy
loudly	monthly	sisterly	unfair	noisy
quickly	weekly	fatherly	unhappy	nosy
quietly	yearly		unhealthy	smelly
safely			unkind	sunny
slowly			unload	muddy
suddenly			unlock	berry
Add **ly** to an adjective to change it to an adverb.	Add **ly** to a noun to change it to a time adverbial.	Add **ly** onto nouns to change them to adjectives.	The prefix **un** means the opposite.	It is used to change a noun to an adjective.

il	s/es	s/es	ies	
fossil	cries	birds	babies	ate
evil	drinks	books	berries	caught
lentil	eats	brushes	ladies	had
gerbil	feels	clothes	puppies	had
nostril	gets	boxes	leaves	ran
stencil	goes	hairs	knives	said
brazil	has	dishes	roofs	swam
until	sees	riches	shelves	thought
pupil	thinks	pushes	wolves	was
tonsil	plants	dresses	wives	swam
	The verb changed from the first person to the third person—the **y** changes to **ies.**	If it ends in **s, ss, x, ch,** or **sh,** add **es.** When the plural creates another syllable, then add **es.**	Plural. When the singular ends in **y,** drop the **y** and add **ies.** It ends in an **f** change to **v** and add **es.**	Irregular past tense verbs.

ei	ei	Contractions	Possessives
ceiling	abseil	he'd	child's
conceive	beige	I've	boy's
deceive	reign	she'll	boys'
receipt	reindeer	they'd	children's
receive	veil	they've	her
deceit	vein	we'll	his
perceive		don't	theirs'
		aren't	girl's
		she's	girls'
		I'm	
Place the **i** before **e** except after **c** when the sound is long.			If the subject is singular, place the apostrophe before the **s**; if it is plural, put the apostrophe after the s.

Homophones

their/there	role/roll	soar/sore	weak/week
pair/pear	blew/blue	toe/tow	meet/meat
eight/ate	tail/tale	to/too/two	flour/flower
right/write	see/sea	tide/tied	for/four
vein/vain	sun/son	waste/waist	grate/great
I/eye	band/banned	bear/bare	fir/fur
new/knew	sew/so	some/sum	wood/would
by/buy/bye	band/banned	rows/rose	maid/made
been/bean	beach/beech	owe/oh	hour/our
whole/hole	be/bee	sum/some	bare/bear
root/route	way/weigh	so/sow	role/roll
scent/sent	wring/ring	not/knot	deer/dear
hour/our	write/right	night/knight	die/dye
won/one	tow/toe	tea/tee	hair/hare
heel/heal	know/no	red/read	mail/male

Contractions

will	are	is	not	have	had
he'll	they're	he's	can't	I've	he'd
I'll	what're	she's	aren't	they've	I'd
she'll	who're	it's	hasn't	we've	she'd
they'll	you're	that's	hadn't	who've	they'd
we'll		there's	wouldn't	you've	we'd
who'll		what's	won't		who'd
you'll		where's	mustn't		you'd

23 CAPTIONS AND SENTENCES

Phase Two Caption and Sentences

Mum is sad.

Cat and dog can dig.

I can see a rat.

A cat can nap.

A pig in a bin.

A fat cat.

A big red bus.

A pin on a map.

It is Sam.

Run to Dad.

Mum is sick.

It is Dad.

It is fun.

Pick up the mug and the cup.

Fill the bucket.

Hug the rabbit and the cat.

Go to bed.

The bug is fat.

Run to the bus.

Phase Three Sentences

Mark had fish and chips on a dish.

Dad has tools in a shed.

I see sixteen trees.

The ship hits the rocks with a thud.

Lots of shops sell chicken.

I am in a rush to get fish and chips.

A man is rich if he has lots of cash.

This weekend I will go camping.

Jim has six silver coins.

I can hear an owl hoot at night.

Nan sits in a rocking chair.

Bow down to the king and queen.

I can hear an owl hoot at night.

Bow down to the king and queen.

It has been hot this year.

Jill has six silver coins.

I can see a pair of boots on the mat.

I got wet in the rain.

Nan sits in the rocking chair.

I can see a pair of boots on the mat.

Stan had a chat with his dad.

Phase Four Sentences
He spent a week in Spain.

It is fun to camp in a green tent.

Milk is good for children's teeth.

I must not tramp on the flowers.

I can hear twigs snapping in the wind.

A drip from the tap drops in the sink.

I kept bumping into things in the dark.

The taps drip into the sink.

The frog jumps in the pond.

I must no stomp on the flowers.

A crab crept into a crack in the rock.

I kept bumping into things in the dark.

The clown did tricks with a chimpanzee.

The bench was cold and wet.

The champ swam thirteen laps in the pool.

The three girls wept.

The crab snaps at the fish.

What is that on the bookshelf?

The pram was under the tree.

The green croc went for a swim in the pond.

I like French food.

The grinch slept on the train.

Phase Five Sentences

She can play the flute.

The boy came to the house to eat cake.

The girl saw a bluebird by the sea.

The boy came to the house to eat some pies.

The old dog took his bone home.

The crayons looked brand new.

She saw a bluebird by the sea.

An elephant stomped on the snake's tail.

The crayons looked new.

The old, grey house looks spooky and haunted.

My nose is running, and I must use a tissue.

I looked at the monkey's claws when it sat on the chimney.

The dog took his bone home.

Should you carry an elephant on your head?

Would you like to wave a magic wand?

Would you crawl into a thorn bush?

I like honey on my bagel.

I think the clouds look like puffs of smoke.

Mrs Blue makes cakes for Mr Yellow.

On Monday, mother will make the turkey for dinner.

I love beef jerky.

The storm will destroy the pyramids and the sphinx in Egypt.

Phase Six Sentences

Grandad tried baling a wedding cake.

Father said, "The train's here early."

The mother went to the park and played with the puppies.

It is unusual to eat smelly cheese while walking in the park.

The space shuttle roared loudly as it took off.

The magician made the rabbit disappear in front of the girl's eyes.

There was a lot of excitement at the dance school's concert.

The wind blew strongly and knocked over a table.

Simon talked louder than Harry, and Joe was the loudest.

The teacher tested each child's spelling.

Jane flew a colourful kite over the white, frothy river.

The bride and groom were the luckiest couple on the island.

The eagle silently swooped down on its prey.

The dragon roared angrily at the brave, young knight.

The penniless girl wanted payment for the entertainment.

The boy's monthly disagreement with his parents started after he crashed his bicycle.

The reindeer fly over Santa's house annually.

The small, hairy gerbil carefully climbed up the metal cage.

I am unclear on the expectations.

The friendly children playfully threw chewy fruit cake at the Christmas elves.

My sister ate six boxes of crunchy, fresh Brazil nuts.

The wolves ran slowly around the park daily.

GLOSSARY

Abbreviation: A shortened form of a word with full stops indicating missing letters.

Accent: The way a language is pronounced.

Adjective: A word that describes a noun.

Adverb: A word that says how, when or where something happens.

Alliteration: Words that begin with the same sound alongside each other or close to each other in a sentence.

Apostrophe: A punctuation mark used to indicate possession or show where letters have been left out.

Auditory Discrimination: The ability to distinguish between different sounds in the environment.

Auditory Figure-Ground Discrimination: The ability to focus on important sounds in a noisy environment.

Auditory Memory: The ability to recall what has been heard.

Auditory Sequencing: The ability to recall words or sounds in order.

Bilateral Integration: The ability for the two hands to work together to perform a task, like holding a piece of paper with one hand while cutting with the other.

Blending: Joining sounds together to form a word.

Blog: An online journal or diary.

CCVC: Words made from a consonant, consonant, vowel, consonant. For example, frog.

Clause: A part of a sentence that contains a subject and a verb.

Collective noun: A word used to describe a group of animals or people.

Comma: A punctuation mark used to separate words or phrases in a sentence.

Command: A sentence that tells someone what to do.

Common Noun: Naming words for ordinary people, places, things, and ideas.

Compound Word: Two words joined together to form a new word.

Conjunction: A word used to connect phrases, words, or clauses in a sentence.

Consonant: All the letters of the alphabet, excluding the vowels.

Consonant Blends: Two or three consonants alongside each other in a word that makes two or three sounds.

Contraction: A word created by joining two words together and leaving out certain letters with an apostrophe to indicate the missing letters.

Co-ordinating Conjunction: A conjunction that joins two main clauses together in a sentence.

CVC: Words: words made from a consonant, vowel, consonant. For example, cat

CVCC: Words made from a consonant, vowel, consonant, consonant. For example, bend

Crossing the Midline: The ability to cross the invisible line that runs from the top of the head down through the middle of the body through the nose.

Decoding: This is the process whereby a child sees and can read a word.

Digraph: Two letters that make one sound.

Diphthong: A digraph where both vowel sounds are heard.

EHCP: Education, Health and Care Plan. This is a plan that is created in conjunction with the local council, it is for children who need more support and additional resources that the school lgenerally do not provide.

Exclamation: A sentence that expresses strong feelings.

Exclamation Mark: The punctuation mark used in an exclamation.

Expanded Noun Phrase: A phrase that consists of a noun and at least one adjective.

Graph: One letter representing one sound

Grapheme: A single letter or group of letters that represent one sound.

HA: Higher ability or attainment pupil, these children should be working at greater depth.

Hand dominance: The consistent use of one preferred hand for repetitive tasks.

Homographs: Words that are spelt the same but have different pronunciations and definitions.

Homophone: Words that sound the same but have different spellings and definitions.

IEP: Individualised Education Program/Plan. It is a plan set out by the teacher to support children who are still struggling after interventions have occurred and therefore need additional support.

LA: Low Attainment or ability pupil sometimes with SEND.

MA: Middle or Medium attainment or ability pupil. The average student in the class that should be working at the expected level.

Morpheme: The smallest complete part of a word.

Noun: A word for a person, place, thing, or idea.

Noun Phrase: A noun and the modifier that distinguishes the noun.

Object: The person, animal or thing referred to by the verb.

Object Manipulation: The ability to use tools like scissors, hairbrushes, and scissors effectively.

Onomatopoeia: Sounds used to mimic objects or animals.

Past tense: A sentence written about something that happened in the past.

Phoneme: A speech sound.

Phoneme Spotter: A worksheet or text containing the sound being taught or learnt.

Plural: Two or more animals, people, or things.

Polysyllabic words: words with more than one syllable.

Prefix: A beginning added on to a root word to change the meaning of the word.

Present tense: A sentence written about something that is happening now.

Pronoun: A word used in place of a noun.

Proper noun: A particular place, person, animal, thing, or idea. Proper nouns begin with capital letters.

Quadgraph: Four letters that make one sound.

Question: A sentence that asks for an answer.

Question mark: The punctuation that indicates the sentence is a question.

Rhyme: Words that have the same last sound.

Rhythm: The timing or beat in a word, sentence, or poem.

Root word: A whole word or part of a word onto which a prefix or suffix can be attached.

Schwa: A vowel sound 'uh.'

Segmenting: Breaking words into their separate sounds.

SEND: Special education needs and disability, these children have specific health or educational needs.

Sensory Processing: The child's ability to interpret the messages he/she receives from their senses.

Sentence: A set of words together that form a complete idea, containing a subject and a verb.

Split digraph: Two letters represent one sound but are separated by a consonant; there are five split digraphs a-e, e-e, u-e, o-e, and i-e.

Statement: A sentence that states something.

Subordinating Conjunction: A conjunction that joins another phrase or clause onto the sentence to add extra information to the main clause.

Suffix: An ending added onto a root word.

Superlative: An adjective or adverb that suggests something is the most of, or the greatest/least of something.

Syllable: They sound like the beat in a word. You can count the syllables by clapping the beat of a word.

Tense: When an action takes place.

Trigraph: Three letters that make one sound.

Unvoiced: The airflow creates the sound.

Verb: A doing word.

Visual Attention: The ability to focus on the important information visually.

Visual Discrimination: The ability to see similarities and differences.

Visual Figure-Ground: The ability to find something on a busy background.

Visual Form Constancy: The understanding that a shape or letter remains the same despite its size or orientation.

Visual Memory: The ability to remember the shape of an object or the objects themselves.

Visual Sequential Memory: The ability to remember objects in order.

Visual Spatial Relationships: Understanding where things are in space and in relation to each other.

Voiced: This sound is made through friction.

Vowel: The letters a, e, i, o, and u and sometimes y

Word: A group of letters together that together have meaning.

REFERENCES

Insert Addy, L (2015) *Speed Up! A kinaesthetic programme to develop fluent handwriting*. UK: LDA.
Byrne, N, (2008) *LCP Phonics Planning, Day by Day Lesson Plans based on Letters and Sounds.* LCP
Budden, Jo (2008) British Councill: Grouping Students, Available at: https://www.teachingenglish.org.uk/article/grouping-students (Accessed 15 May 2021)
(2021) Consortium the education supply people, Available at: https://www.consortiumeducation.com/ (Accessed: 10 April 2021).
Cripps, C. and Cox, R. (1996) *Joining the ABC*. Wisbech, Cambs: LDA
(2021) Dyslexia Reading Well, Available at:https://www.dyslexia-reading-well.com/support-files/the-44-phonemes-of-english.pdf (Accessed: 21 April 2021)
(2021) edu-k About Educational Kinesiology, Available at: https://braingym.org.uk/about-edu-k/ (Accessed: 7 April 2021)
(2021) Games Grown and Picked by Bananagrams. Available at: https://bananagrams.com/blogs/news/how-to-play-bananagrams-instructions-for-getting-started (Accessed: 17 March 2021)
(2021) Gov. uk, Department for Education. Available at: https://www.gov.uk/government/publications/phonics-teaching-materials-core-criteria-and-self-assessment/validation-of-systematic-synthetic-phonics-programmes-supporting-documentation (Accessed:20 May 2021)
(2021) 123 HomeSchool 4 Me Available at: https://www.123homeschool4me.com/kindergarten-word-family-sliders_24/ (Accessed: 21 March 2021)
Kelly, Melissa. (2020, August 27). Creating Effective Lesson Objectives. Retrieved https://www.thoughtco.com/lesson-objectives-that-produce-results-7763
(2021) Kid Sense: Visual Perception Available at: https://childdevelopment.com.au/areas-of-concern/visual-perception/ (Accessed 5 April 2021)
(2007) *Letters and Sounds: Principles and Practice of High-Quality Phonics, Six-phase Teaching Programme*. Department for Education and Skills
Lloyd, S. (1992) *The Phonics Handbook*. Chigwell: Jolly Learning Ltd.
Lundberg, I. Olofsson, A and Wall, S. (1980) Reading and Spelling Skills in the First School Years Predicted from Phonemic Awareness Skills in Kindergarten. *Scandinavian Journal of Psychology*, 21,159-173.
Masterson, J. Stuart, M. Dixon, M. &Lovejoy, S. (2003) Children's Printed Word Database. Economic and Social Research Council Funded Project, R00023406.
McGuinness, D. *Early Reading Instruction: What Science Really Tells Us About How to Teach Reading*
(2021) Mighty Writer, Available at: https://www.mightywriter.co.uk/ (Accessed: 11 April 2021)
(2021) Muse Printables, Available at: https://museprintables.com/c/writing-templates/category/animal/ (Accessed: 18 August 2021)
(2021) OxfordOwl, Available at: https://support.oxfordowl.co.uk/teacher-support/school- subscriptions/subscription-guidance/nelson-handwriting/ (Accessed 12 April 2021)
Parfetti, C. Beck, I. Bell, L and Hughes (1987) *Phonemic Knowledge and Learning to Read are Reciprocal: A Longitudinal Study of First Grade Children.* Merrill-Palmer Quarterly, 33, 283-39.
(2021) PhonicsPlay Available at: https://www.phonicsplay.co.uk/ (Accessed: 06 March 2021).
(2021) PuzzleMaker Discovery Education Available at https://www.puzzlemaker.discoveryeducation.com/ (Accessed: 3 May 2021)
(2021) Reading Elephant. Available at: https://www.readingelephant.com/phonics-books-overview/ (Accessed: 27 March 2021)
Rice, M. (1985) *Play Together Learn Together*. London: Rainbow Books
(2021) Sarah's Teaching Snippets Available at: https://sarahsnippets.com/phonemic-awareness-intervention-pack/ (Accessed 2 April 2021)
Share, D.L. Jorm, A.F. MacLean and Matthews, R (1984) Sources of Individual Differences in Reading Achievement. *Journal of Educational Psychology*, 76, 1309-1324r.
(2021) PhonicBooks, Available at: https://www.phonicbooks.co.uk/shop/ (Accessed: 19 May 2021)
(2021) Smart Kids, Available at: https://www.smartkids.co.uk/ (Accessed: 10 April 2021)

Strategies for Improving Literacy Skills and Students with CVI. https://www.perkins.org/assets/downloads/webinars/presentation/strategies-for-improving-literacy.pdf
(2021) Start Here Parenting, Available at: https://startthereparents.com/dysgraphia-symptoms/ (Accessed 10 May 2021).
(2021) https://www.flickr.com/photos/whiteafrican/731467843
(2021) Sweet Clip Art, Available at: https://sweetclipart.com/ (Acessesed:8 April 2021)
(2021) Talk for Writing, Available at: https://www.talk4writing.com/ (Accessed: 15 May 2021)
(2021) The Anonymous OT Available at: https://theanonymousot.com/2018/07/05/10-go-to-games- to-work-on-visual-perception/ (Accessed 9 April 2021)
(2021) Teacher's Takeout Available at: http://www.teacherstakeout.com/2015/02/44-sounds-of-english-language-freebie.html?m=1 (Accessed 27 March 2021).
(2021) Teach with Laughter, Available at: https://teachwithlaughter.blogspot.com/2017/08/reading-strategies.html (Accessed: 13 May 2021)
(2021) Teroes, Available at: https://www.teroes.com/2019/03/what-is-dyspraxia.html (Accessed 14 May 2021)
(2021) The THRASSinstitute Available at: https://www.thrass.com.au/ (Accessed 06 March 2021).
(2013) *The 2014 Primary National Curriculum in England, Key Stages 1&2Framework Document.* Shurville Publishing.
(2021) The Tricky Word Song Available at: https://www.youtube.com/watch?v=TvMyssfAUx0 (Accessed: 06 March 2021)
(2021) Twinkl, Available at: https://www.twinkl.co.uk/blog/plenary-ideas (Accessed: 15 May 2021)
(2021) Understood, Available at: https://www.understood.org/en/learning-thinking-differences/child-learning-disabilities/dysgraphia/difference-between-dysgraphia-dyspraxia (Accessed at 14 May 2021)
(2021) Welcome to MyCuteGraphics! Available at: https://www.mycutegraphics.com/ (Accessed:06 March 2021).
Wernham, S. Lloyd, S. (2010) *Phonics Teacher's Book.* Chigwell: Jolly Learning Ltd (2021) https://www.flickr.com/photos/pennuja/5931765266
(2021) Wiki How to do anything. How to Play Boggle. Available at: https://www.wikihow.com/Play-Boggle#:~:text=%Two0Setting%Two0Up%Two0%Two0One%Two0Put%Two0the%Two0game,run%Two0out%Two0of%Two0sand%Two0in%Two0three...%Two0More%Two0 (Accessed 07 March 2021)

PICTURE ACKNOWLEDGEMENTS

(2021) https://en.wikipedia.org/wiki/Charcoal_(art). By Stephhzz - Own work, CC BY-SA 3.0, https://commons.wikimedia.org/w/index.php?curid=11728347

(2021) Free Kindergarten Teacher and Parent Resources. https://www.kindergartenteacherresources.com/spot-difference/ (Accessed 5 May 2021)

(2021) Marco Verch. https://foto.wuestenigel.com/jenga-tower-game-with-wooden-blocks-on-white-background/

(2021) Free images Live https://www.freeimageslive.co.uk/free_stock_image/colorful-bricks-jpg

(2021) By Original image by Whitney Waller, red lines added - connect-the-dots, CC BY-SA 2.0, https://commons.wikimedia.org/w/index.php?curid=45762476

(2021) By Maciozik - Own work, CC BY-SA 3.0, https://commons.wikimedia.org/w/index.php?curid=19732202

(2021) By Maciozik - Own work, CC BY-SA 3.0, https://commons.wikimedia.org/w/index.php?curid=19732202

(2021) By Udjat - Own work, CC BY-SA 3.0, https://commons.wikimedia.org/w/index.php?curid=10576717

(2021) By No machine-readable author provided. Peng assumed (based on copyright claims). - No machine-readable source provided. Own work assumed (based on copyright claims)., CC BY-SA 3.0, https://commons.wikimedia.org/w/index.php?curid=27659

(2021) By Michael Rivera - Own work, CC BY-SA 3.0, https://commons.wikimedia.org/w/index.php?curid=23824885

(2021) By Shritwod - Own work, CC0, https://commons.wikimedia.org/w/index.php?curid=74999741

By Nevit Dilmen - Own work, CC BY-SA 3.0, https://commons.wikimedia.org/w/index.php?curid=3775216

By Nevit Dilmen - Own work, CC BY-SA 3.0, https://commons.wikimedia.org/w/index.php?curid=3775221

(2021) By Mokkie - Own work, CC BY-SA 4.0, https://commons.wikimedia.org/w/index.php?curid=45119586

By Jim Pennucci from Hope, USA - Painting, CC BY 2.0, https://commons.wikimedia.org/w/index.php?curid=19451952

By Sue Clark - Flickr: Jack and Jill, Public Domain, https://commons.wikimedia.org/w/index.php?curid=16141467

By Tim Pierce - originally posted to Flickr as lost, CC BY 2.0, https://commons.wikimedia.org/w/index.php?curid=4614902

(2021) File: Two monks tangram paradox.svg. https://en.wikipedia.org/wiki/File:Two_monks_tangram_paradox.svg

ABOUT THE AUTHOR

Kerry Dickinson has been teaching for more than twenty years in private and public schools both in the UK and overseas. She studied Primary School Teaching, Early Years Education and English Literature and Language. She has worked in EYFS, Keystage 1 and Keystage 2 and has an excellent grasp of the whole English Curriculum.

As a child Kerry was touched by how hard it was for some children to learn to read, write and spell. This fascination later developed into a passion that fuelled endless hours of research and study as she tried to find ways to help pupils overcome difficulties and develop a love of language. Later when Kerry started working with student teachers she felt moved to share this knowledge and what started as a short pamphlet to help her trainee teachers quickly developed into this book.

Printed in Great Britain
by Amazon

66261636R00104